Microeconomics

To Josette

Microeconomics for Public Policy

Helping the Invisible Hand

CLAUDE HENRY

CLARENDON PRESS · OXFORD

Oxford University Press, Walton Street, Oxford OX2 6DP

Oxford New York Toronto
Delhi Bombay Calcutta Madras Karachi
Petaling Jaya Singapore Hong Kong Tokyo
Nairobi Dar es Salaam Cape Town
Melbourne Auckland
and associated companies in
Ibadan

Oxford is a trade mark of Oxford University Press

Published in the United States
by Oxford University Press, New York

First published 1989
First issued in paperback 1991

British Library Cataloguing in Publication Data
Henry C. (Claude)
Microeconomics for public policy: helping
the invisible hand
1. Microeconomics
I Title
338.5
ISBN 0–19–877288–2
ISBN 0–19–877327–7 (Pbk)

Library of Congress Cataloging in Publication Data
Henry, C. (Claude)
Microeconomics for public policy: helping the invisible hand
C. Henry.

Bibliography   Includes index.
1. Microeconomics.   2. Economic policy.   I. Title.
HB172.H52   1989   338.5—dc19   88-32227
ISBN 0–19–877288–2
ISBN 0–19–877327–7 (Pbk)

Printed and bound in
Great Britain by Biddles Ltd,
Guildford and King's Lynn

Acknowledgements

I wish to thank Michel Balinski, Patrick Bolton, Paul Champsaur, Jacques Crémer, Roger Guesnerie, and Jean-Charles Rochet for valuable discussions on various parts of the manuscript. I have also benefited from students' comments at Ecole Polytechnique (Paris) and at Lausanne University. I feel specially indebted to Nancy Crémer who translated a first draft written in French and who did much to improve successive versions in English. I am grateful to Marie-Hélène Ponroy for outstanding secretarial assistance.

Contents

Appendix 131

Introduction

The goal of this book is to show how concepts and methods of microeconomics—often very simple ones—can illuminate important issues of public affairs. The issues themselves tend to be complicated, sometimes to the point of confusion, and the controversies that they frequently spawn seldom help to clarify what is at stake. It is no paradox that this very complexity creates the necessity of simple models. But there are dangers. Simplification risks oversimplification, and common sense can be as misleading as an excess of sophistication. One needs models that are, in the words of Albèrt Einstein, 'as simple as possible, but no simpler': as simple as possible so as not to obscure the very issues one seeks to clarify, but no simpler, for fear that one's conclusions become a mere artefact of the model itself.

Clearly, it is not possible in a book of modest size to consider more than a sample of issues. Their selection has proceeded from two criteria:

1. that they are of significance in developed economies, like those of most European and North American countries;
2. that they lead to the introduction and the utilization of concepts and methods general enough to be of broad use in economic analysis.

Applications are introduced along with methods throughout the book. The following four examples give an idea of the nature of these applications and how they fit in with the main themes of the successive chapters.

The performance of the Channel Tunnel will be highly dependent on the way the traffic is managed at both ends of the tunnel. What should be the capacity of the terminals? How much should different kinds of vehicles, at different times of the day and year, be charged? These points are crucial. It is impossible to deal with them without making good use of the economics of public goods.

The Commission of the European Communities put it very clearly: 'Each mode of transportation, and, within each of these modes, each category of users, must cover through its own means the totality of costs which are imputable to it. This precludes all aid from public funds as well as all subsidy of one activity by another.' This seems to make good sense. The Law Lords felt so when they ruled out the 'Fares Fair' scheme set by London Transport to attract new customers: London Transport 'must balance its books', and that scheme made it impossible. In the same vein, a special committee on public transport warned the Prime Minister of France against cross-subsidies. But good sense may be misleading. In matters where so many economic agents and variables are involved, one cannot disregard economic models that incorporate in a systematic way interactions that are beyond the reach of simple arguments. And these models support an integrated approach to the design of taxes and of pricing schemes for public services: they do not support the compartmentalized approach which looks so reasonable at first sight.

In order to make its competitors more accommodating, it is not unusual for a firm voluntarily to restrict its clientele; for example, it might refrain from developing its distribution network, or direct its advertising only to a narrow category of customers. Such restrictive practices should be opposed, it seems, by public policies. They do, indeed, soften the competition between firms that are active in the market. But, the softer is active competition, the more constraining is potential competition. It is thus essential to correctly assess what kind of competition will prevail in order not to implement the wrong policy.

The Medical School of the University of California at Davis has two admission programmes: a general one and a special one, the latter aiming at a better representation of disadvantaged students in the school, such as black and Mexican–American students. Having been rejected under the general programme, despite marks that would have gained him easy admission under the special programme, a white applicant filed a suit against the University of California; he alleged that the special programme 'operated to exclude him from the school on the basis of his race'. Eventually the case came before the Supreme Court of the United States. While this is primarily a legal case, economics can fruitfully contribute to its analysis. Indeed, the university is faced with a problem of resource allocation under imperfect information. The discrimination devices it uses—a scale of marks within each programme and limited access to one of the two programmes—aim at obviating the lack of direct information about the potential medical abilities of the applicants. Obviously, the racial content of the word 'discrimination' comes first to mind. The relevance of its economic content should not however be underestimated; and the Justices themselves have taken some steps in that direction.

Corresponding to the order in which these examples are introduced, the structure of the book is described more explicitly as follows. Chapters 1 and 2 deal with the theory of public goods and its main applications. Since a public good is not divided into units that are consumed separately by different people, but is used by all in common, one cannot expect individual initiative and the usual market mechanisms to suffice for its management. Which public goods to provide and how to finance them are the central questions here. They raise issues of efficiency and equity which, although they have their counterparts in the economics of ordinary private goods, require a different approach, one that leads to original solutions. This is the subject of Chapter 1. In Chapter 2 the regulation of crowding is examined, the objective being to minimize the negative effects resulting from the interactions between the different users of a public good.

It is often not possible to finance public goods with specific contributions paid directly by their users. Providing and financing those goods then becomes part of the management of public finance, which is dealt with in Chapters 3 and 4. Here one confronts a fundamental problem of incentives. For example, setting taxes changes the incentives of economic agents, causing them to misallocate valuable resources. Minimizing the resulting waste, while raising enough public money in a way deemed equitable, is the central objective. The approach is of a 'second-best' nature: being unable to eliminate all waste, one seeks to minimize it. Second-best models are present in a wide range of areas in economics; in Chapters 3 and 4, we restrict ourselves to the domain of taxation and public service pricing.

It may be the case that, of two firms competing in the same market, one is more efficient than the other, because its products are cheaper to produce and are of better quality. The firm is a natural monopoly. In Chapter 5 we investigate ways out of the following dilemma: if both firms are active in the market, that is if both firms produce, resources are wasted; but if the natural monopoly is the sole producer, it is led to abuse its position to the detriment of the consumers. One solution might be to turn the natural monopoly into a public monopoly serving the consumers' interests. A consideration of how this public monopoly should then be run is given in Chapters 3 and 4. When this solution is impracticable and the natural monopoly is a firm seeking to maximize its profit, can its appetites be contained by means other than wasteful competition? This question is answered by examining the extent to which threat of entry by a potential competitor leads the natural monopoly to behave in a way more favourable to the consumers than it does either in the absence of any competition or even in the presence of a competitor active in the market.

It would seem that the only aim of discriminating between customers is to increase the producer's profit. In Chapter 6 we show that this view is mistaken: under certain conditions, discrimination makes all users of a public service better off than they can best be without discrimination, as in Chapters 3 and 4. Discrimination can take the form of self-selection: the same possibilities of choice are offered to all, but they are designed to sort out different categories of users. Discrimination can also be based on individual characteristics that are easy to verify, like age or family size; then some possibilities are accessible only to some predetermined categories. The conjunction of these two forms of discrimination is in everyone's interest in certain kinds of situation, and is highly controversial in others; hence the importance of being able to have a sure diagnosis.

Section A1 of the Appendix is meant for the readers who have no previous knowledge of microeconomics: it is an introduction to what is both necessary and sufficient to an understanding of the content of the book, except for Sections 4.3 and 6.3. These two sections—the knowledge of which is not necessary for reading the rest of the book—require a more advanced knowledge of the microeconomics of consumer behaviour, which is provided in Sections A2 and A3 of the Appendix.

There are no mathematical prerequisites other than a familiarity with the very process of formalization and logical analysis, and a reasonable knowledge of calculus, i.e. of functions, concavity, limits, continuity, partial derivatives, and first-order maximization conditions.

1

From Land Use to Peak Pricing: Managing Public Goods

1. Limits of the Invisible Hand

Adam Smith himself refers to limits of the invisible hand in the following terms:

> The third and last duty of a sovereign or commonwealth is that of erecting and maintaining those public institutions and those public works, which, though they may be in the highest degree advantageous to a great society, are, however, of such a nature, that the profit could never repay the expense to any individual or small number of individuals, and which it therefore cannot be expected that any individual or small number of individuals should erect or maintain.[1]

This concern of Adam Smith is at least as pertinent to the twentieth century as it was to the eighteenth. Let us consider, for example, a community in the suburbs of a large city that envisages reopening for passengers a rail line linking it to the city centre. This would allow the residents of the community who must commute regularly to the city to avoid traffic problems. To put the infrastructure of the rail line back into working condition would involve a fixed cost; let C be the amount of that fixed cost. Once the line is running, there would be a cost of operating the trains; let the average cost per passenger-kilometre be constant and equal to c. Spending C

---

[1] *An Enquiry into the Nature and Causes of the Wealth of Nations* (1776), bk. V, ch. 1. It is in bk. IV, ch. 2, that one can find the famous passage: '[The individual] generally, indeed, neither intends to promote the public interest, nor knows how much he is promoting it. By preferring the support of domestic to that of foreign industry, he intends only his own security; and by directing that industry in such a manner as its produce may be of the greatest value, he intends only his own gain, and he is in this, as in many other cases, led by an invisible hand to promote an end which was no part of his intention. Nor is it always the worse for the society that it was no part of it. By pursuing his own interest he frequently promotes that of the society more effectually than when he really intends to promote it.'

to render the infrastructure usable allows each interested resident the chance to travel on the line for a cost c per kilometre. Travelling on the line is a private good, which benefits only the person who is travelling. On the other hand, the possibility of getting this private good at cost c per unit is a public good, which benefits all the potential users: it is available to all of them once it is available to any of them.

How to pay for the cost C of providing the public good? At first glance the answer would seem simple: charge a fare p which is high enough—necessarily higher than c—to raise the revenue required to cover both fixed and operating costs. But this may prove impossible if the demand for rail services decreases too fast as p increases, which may very well happen even if the line is worth reopening. As Jean-Baptiste Say wrote in 1828, 'the costs of the construction of a canal, even the indispensable costs, can be such that the fees for the right to navigate would not be sufficient to pay off the costs, even though the advantages which a nation might draw from the canal would be greatly superior to these costs.'[2]

What can be done? Fo Jules Dupuit, the 'solution rests on this general principle: that one must demand as a price for the service provided not only that which it costs to provide, but a sum commensurate with the importance it represents to the receiver'.[3] This is all very well, but how does one discover this importance and charge the sum that can be assigned to it? And what about the interaction between all those who are using the same public good?

Man is not the only one to produce public goods: nature has preceded him. Those public goods provided by nature raise the same fundamental problems. For instance, why are certain kinds of whales disappearing? Because they are 'over-fished', meaning that no one fisherman is motivated to limit his catch so that a sufficient population is maintained to ensure an adequate level of reproduction of

[2] *Cours complet d'économie politique pratique* (1828), pt. 7, ch. 24. In ch. 22, regarding the 'benefit resulting from a bridge in the middle of a town', Say writes: 'A tollbooth on the bridge would give only an imperfect idea of the benefit the public draws from free passage, for a tollbooth gives an idea of the value of the bridge for those who can pay the toll, but gives no idea of the service provided for those who are unable to pay.'

[3] 'De l'influence des péages sur l'utilité des voies de communication', *Annales des Ponts et Chaussées* (1849). Léon Walras discusses the solution proposed by Jules Dupuit in Lesson 41, 'Des tarifs et du monopole', of his *Eléments d'économie politique pure* (1877).

the animals. This level is a public good for all fishermen. Yet, without being guaranteed some kind of reciprocity, no individual fisherman is inclined to pay for the public good by restraining his catch.

It seems, then, that one cannot expect individual initiative and ordinary market mechanisms to suffice for efficiency when the management of a public good is involved, anyone being able to enjoy the whole of the good without preventing anyone else from enjoying it as well. Consequently, it seems necessary to establish a social contract between all those who are interested in the public good at stake, so that, for example, the fixed cost of a public service could be covered or the reproduction of the whales could be assured (to refer to our two previous examples).

The necessity for this social contract was envisioned with great lucidity by Knut Wicksell as early as 1896:

The actual scope of the public service is not determined by the evaluation of the single individual, but by that of all members of the group. Equality between the marginal utility of public goods and their price cannot, therefore, be established by the single individual, but must be secured by consultation between him and all other individuals or their delegates. How is such consultation to be arranged so that the goal may be realized? . . . as I see it, this is precisely the question which ought to be decided.[4]

2. Efficiency and Equity: Fundamental Landmarks

A town envisages installing a television cable system for its area, ensuring reception of television signals through a central public equipment rather than a number of different private equipments.

Let us first consider what happens if the cable system is not installed. The inhabitants of the town use private equipments in the form of individual antennae, the size of which we will assume to be proportional to the number of stations received. Let x^i be the size of the antenna installed by inhabitant i, each inhabitant making his own decision on the size of his antenna, i.e. on the number of stations he receives. Let y^i be the quantity of all other goods and services that i consumes, along with x^i.

It may seem odd to speak of 'the quantity' of a set of goods. In fact,

---

[4] 'Ein neues Prinzip der gerechten Besteuerung', in *Finanztheoretische Untersuchungen*, translated as 'A New Principle of Just Taxation', by J. M. Buchanan in Musgrave and Peacock (1958).

if the production and consumption of antennae do not occupy a place in the economy such that they would significantly influence the prices of the other goods and services, we can use these prices to aggregate them into one composite good; moreover, we can measure this composite good in such a way that its price is equal to 1; it then plays the role of numeraire in the economy.[5] Our attention is thus focused on two goods. One is described precisely, according to our aims in this study. The other is composite; indeed, we do not need a detailed description of the goods in the economy to pursue our main objective in this chapter. Then x^i and y^i designate the respective quantities of these two goods that inhabitant i—from now on we will call him agent i—chooses to consume; we will say that (x^i, y^i) is his consumption bundle.

How does i choose a consumption bundle? We assume that his preferences can be represented by a utility function U^i, defined on the bundles (x^i, y^i). We assume, moreover, that U^i is increasing in each of the variables on which it depends, is quasi-concave, and is differentiable; these three assumptions will be retained throughout the book.[6]

Endowed with an amount R^i of numeraire, which is his initial income, i maximizes U^i subject to the constraint

$$px^i + y^i = R^i. \tag{1.1}$$

This is a budget constraint: having R^i to spend, i considers those bundles (x^i, y^i) that cost R^i at the prices p and 1 which he is facing. (p is the price of the unit element of an antenna, i.e. the price per station received.) Among such bundles, he chooses one he prefers, i.e. one that maximizes U^i.

The first-order necessary condition for the maximization of U^i under the constraint (1.1) is

$$\pi^i(x^i, y^i) = p, \tag{1.2}$$

where π^i indicates i's marginal rate of substitution of the second good for the first good (calculated at the consumption bundle (x^i, y^i)), i.e.

$$\pi^i(x^i, y^i) = \frac{\partial U^i / \partial x^i}{\partial U^i / \partial y^i}.$$

[5] When a particular good plays the role of numeraire in an economy, that is, when its price is equal to 1, all prices are then expressed in terms of this numeraire: if the price of a good is p, 1 unit of this good is worth p units of the numeraire. We are careful to use the word 'numeraire' and not the word 'money'; the latter covers a range of functions, that of measuring a unit of value being only one among many.

[6] On the representation of preferences by utility functions and on the properties of such functions, see Section A1 of the Appendix.

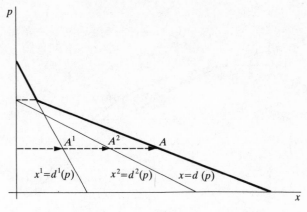

F$_{\text{IG}}$. 1.1

When possible, the elimination of y^i between (1.1) and (1.2) and the resolution in x^i of the equation thus obtained yields the demand function

$$x^i = d^i(p, R^i),\qquad(1.3)$$

which is more simply written

$$x^i = d^i(p),$$

since R^i is here a fixed parameter.

At each level of the price p, the quantities $x^i = d^i(p)$ demanded by all the concerned economic agents i—let N be their number—can be added together, and their sum is the aggregate demand

$$d(p) = \sum_{i=1}^{N} d^i(p).\qquad(1.4)$$

On Figure 1.1, which is drawn for $N = 2$, the addition of $d_1(p)$ and $d_2(p)$ is done parallel to the x axis, i.e. horizontally.

To avoid all unnecessary complication,[7] we will assume that the cost of production of the antennae is proportional to the quantity produced (constant returns) and that they are sold at a price $\bar{p}$ equal to the unit cost of their production (competitive market). Figure 1.2, drawn for an economy composed of two agents ($i = 1,2$), permits us to compare two states in the space of utilities U^1 and U^2: an initial

---

[7] Which would only cloud the presentation of the points at issue in this section. On cost functions and on the concepts of competitive firms and competitive markets, see Section A1 in the Appendix.

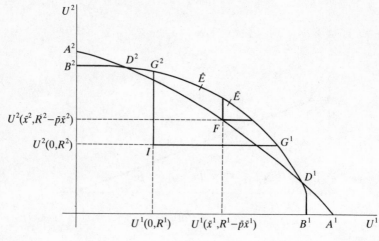

Fɪɢ. 1.2

state I without television, and a state $\bar{F}$ which results from the
decisions— taken individually by the agents i in response to the price
$\bar{p}$—to acquire the quantities $\bar{x}^i$ such that $\bar{x}^i = d^i(\bar{p})$. $\bar{F}$ is on the utility
possibility frontier $A^1 A^2$. Indeed, the utility possibility frontier cor-
responds, in the space of utilities, to the set of Pareto-efficient
allocations of the economy.[8]

Instead of individual antennae, the cable system comprises a collective antenna and transmission cables. This collective installation
is a public good in the economy that we are considering. We will
measure the size x of this public good as the number of stations
received. This collective mode of reception is advantageous if its cost,
which we write as $C(x)$ and suppose to be differentiable, is sufficiently
low to compensate for the rigidity of its operation.[9] This rigidity
springs from the fact that the number of stations received cannot be
modulated according to individual preferences. As is characteristic of
a public good, this number is the same for all. One is thus left with
the question of what size x to install, i.e. what level of public good to

[8] Pareto-efficient allocations are also called 'socially efficient allocations', or
'Pareto-optimal allocations', or 'socially optimal allocations', or 'Pareto optima'; see
Section A1 in the Appendix.
[9] In Fig. 1.2, we see that between D^1 and D^2 the collective technology, or public
good, is preferable to the private system: the advantage of cost more than compensates
the rigidity of operation.

produce,[10] and also how to distribute the contributions towards the cost of production $C(x)$.

Let us suppose that the level chosen is x and the contribution by agent i is t^i. Then

$$y^i = R^i - t^i \tag{1.1'}$$

and

$$\pi^i(x, y^i) = \frac{\partial U^i/\partial x}{\partial U^i/\partial y^i}$$

where $\pi^i(x, y^i)$ is i's marginal rate of substitution of the private good (at level y^i) for the public good (at level x). The marginal rate can be considered either as the maximum amount agent i is willing to pay for a marginal increase in x, or the minimum compensation he will accept for a marginal decrease in x. More precisely, if x is increased (resp. decreased) by dx and if y^i is simultaneously decreased (resp. increased) by $\pi^i dx$, U^i does not vary.

Let us consider the interpretation in terms of willingness to pay[11]—nothing would be changed in what follows if we considered the interpretation in terms of compensation, instead. At each level x offered, the individual $\pi^i(x, y^i)$ can be added together. Their sum over the N concerned agents is the total, or collective, willingness to pay:

$$\pi(x) = \sum_{i=1}^{N} \pi^i(x, y^i), \tag{1.4'}$$

which depends not only on x but also on each y^i, $\pi(x)$ being a shorthand notation for $\pi(x, y^1, \ldots, y^N)$. On Figure 1.3, which is drawn for $N = 2$, the addition of $\pi^1(x, y^1)$ and $\pi^2(x, y^2)$ must be done parallel to the π axis, hence vertically.

Comparing $\pi(x)$ with the marginal cost $c(x) = dC(x)/dx$ of production of the public good,[12] we see that, if

$$\pi(x) > c(x),$$

---

[10] In the case of the rail line (Section 1 above), only two levels were considered: do nothing, or reopen the line. But in that case too, we might have considered a larger choice. It might for example have been possible to conceive different designs for the renovated infrastructure—the more costly a design, the higher the maximum speed permitted to the trains.

[11] To lighten the terminology, we will not continue to repeat 'maximum' or 'minimum'. In addition, remember that, until indicated otherwise, willingness to pay and compensation correspond to marginal variations.

[12] In the case of constant returns $C(x) = cx$ and $c(x)$ is equal to the constant c.

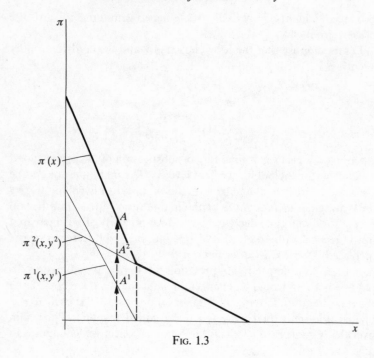

Fig. 1.3

then it is socially advantageous to increase x (by a quantity dx), since it is possible to finance the cost of this increase $(c(x)dx)$ in asking of each participant i a contribution less than the maximum he is willing to pay $(\pi^i(x)dx)$. Similarly, if

$$\pi(x) < c(x),$$

then it is socially advantageous to decrease x $(dx < 0)$, since the savings that result $(-c(x)dx)$ exceed the sum of the compensations $(-\Sigma_{i=1}^{N}\pi^i(x)dx)$ demanded by the agents for this decrease.

To summarize, the condition

$$\sum_{i=1}^{N} t^i = C(x) \tag{1.5}$$

expresses budget balance: the cost of production of the public good must be exactly covered by the contributions of the beneficiaries. As for the condition

$$\pi(x) = c(x), \tag{1.6}$$

which is called the Samuelson condition (Samuelson 1954), it is necessary for efficiency. When this condition does not hold, a marginal modification of x, either an increase or a decrease, is desirable, since the cost of such a change in x is either smaller or greater than the total amount that the concerned agents are willing to pay for the change.

Up to now we have dealt with the case of a single public good. The approach can be generalized to the case of a set of public goods for which one would have to make co-ordinated decisions, for reasons of technology or budget. Such is the case of a town which must decide on the sizes of various kinds of facilities to be included in a sports complex that it is planning, or a public transport authority which must decide simultaneously on the frequency and comfort of the vehicles it puts into circulation. These qualities of service are public goods for the potential users. To carry the previous approach to this more general case, it suffices to consider a vector $\mathbf{x}$ having as many dimensions, K, as there are public goods under simultaneous consideration. The condition (1.5) of budget balance is not changed: t^i is the contribution of agent i to the cost $C(\mathbf{x})$ of producing the quantities $x_1 \ldots, x_K$ of the different public goods simultaneously being planned. The Samuelson condition becomes a collection of Samuelson conditions, one for each public good k:

$$\sum_{i=1}^{N} \pi_k^i(\mathbf{x}, y^i) = c_k(\mathbf{x}) \tag{1.7}$$

where

$$\pi_k^i(\mathbf{x}, y^i) = \frac{\partial U^i / \partial x_k}{\partial U^i / \partial y^i}$$

is the marginal rate of substitution of the private good for the public good k, the level of all the other public goods being fixed, and where

$$c_k(\mathbf{x}) = \frac{\partial C}{\partial x_k}$$

is the marginal cost of producing the public good k.

Along with the condition of budget balance, the Samuelson conditions determine within the space of utilities U^i the utility possibility frontier of the economy with public goods, corresponding to the set of Pareto-efficient allocations for this economy. In Figure 1.2 this appears as the curve B^1B^2. To describe this transition from the space of allocations $(\mathbf{x}, t^1, \ldots, t^N)$ to the space of utility levels

$(U^1, \ldots, U^N)$, the best method is to prove the Samuelson conditions, following the usual schema of proof regarding Pareto-optimal conditions. Samuelson conditions do, in fact, result from the maximization of the utility of one of the agents involved:

$$\max U^1(\mathbf{x}, R^1 - t^1)$$

subject to the conditions

$$U^j(\mathbf{x}, R^j - t^j) = u^j, \qquad j = 2, \ldots, N$$

and

$$\sum_{i=1}^{N} t^i - C(\mathbf{x}) = 0.$$

The first $N - 1$ conditions fix at predetermined levels u^j the utilities of all of the other agents involved, and the last is the condition of budget balance. The maximization is conducted with respect to the coordinates x_k of $\mathbf{x}$ and the t^i. Indicating by $\mu^j (j = 2, \ldots, N)$, and λ the multipliers associated with the constraints, we obtain the Lagrangean

$$\mathscr{L} = U^1(\mathbf{x}, R^1 - t^1) + \sum_{j=2}^{N} \mu^j U^j(\mathbf{x}, R^j - t^j) + \lambda \left\{ \sum_{i=1}^{N} t^i - C(\mathbf{x}) \right\}.$$

By setting to zero the derivatives of the Lagrangean with respect to the variables x_k $(k = 1, \ldots, K)$ and t^i $(i = 1, \ldots, N)$, we obtain the first-order necessary conditions for the constrained maximization of U^1:

$$\frac{\partial \mathscr{L}}{\partial x_k} = \frac{\partial U^1}{\partial x_k} + \sum_{j=2}^{N} \mu^j \frac{\partial U^j}{\partial x_k} - \lambda c_k(\mathbf{x}) = 0$$

$$\frac{\partial \mathscr{L}}{\partial t^1} = -\frac{\partial U^1}{\partial y^1} + \lambda = 0$$

$$\frac{\partial \mathscr{L}}{\partial t^j} = -\mu^j \frac{\partial U^j}{\partial y^j} + \lambda = 0, \qquad j = 2, \ldots, N.$$

By eliminating λ and μ^j, the first K conditions become

$$\frac{\partial U^1/\partial x_k}{\partial U^1/\partial y^1} + \sum_{j=2}^{N} \frac{\partial U^j/\partial x_k}{\partial U^j/\partial y^j} = c_k(\mathbf{x})$$

or

$$\sum_{i=1}^{N} \pi_k^i(\mathbf{x}, y^i) = c_k(\mathbf{x}).$$

If the cost function C is convex, Samuelson conditions are also sufficient. Along with the condition of budget balance, they characterize the utility possibility frontier. Still, they do not select a particular point on this frontier. The choice of such a point is an integral part of the collective decision to be made, and constitutes for the collectivity a degree of freedom[13] in a distribution policy.

It is therefore useful to have available instruments as explicit as possible to evaluate the distributive consequences, between the N concerned agents, of the choice of a particular point E on the efficiency frontier. These instruments correspond to the transition from I to E and are thus of a global nature as opposed to the conditions of efficiency, which are of a marginal nature. We will denote them as ϕ^i and S.

For each $i = 1, \ldots, N$, ϕ^i is a real function of $\mathbf{x}$ defined by

$$U^i\{\mathbf{x}, R^i - \phi^i(\mathbf{x})\} = U^i(0, R^i).$$

If $\phi^i(\mathbf{x}) \geq 0$, that is if $\mathbf{x}$ represents an advantage for i, then $\phi^i(\mathbf{x})$ is the maximum amount i is willing to pay to have $\mathbf{x}$.

If $\phi^i(\mathbf{x}) < 0$, that is if $\mathbf{x}$ represents a disadvantage for i, then $-\phi^i(\mathbf{x})$ is the minimum compensation that must be given to i to counterbalance $\mathbf{x}$.

Also, S is a real function of $\mathbf{x}$ defined by

$$S(\mathbf{x}) = \sum_{i=1}^{N} \phi^i(\mathbf{x}) - C(\mathbf{x}). \tag{1.8}$$

$S(\mathbf{x})$ is the collective surplus generated by the production of $\mathbf{x}$.

Let us consider an allocation $(\mathbf{x}, t^1, \ldots, t^N)$, efficient or not, that is balanced, in the sense that the financial contributions t^i cover the cost of production $C(\mathbf{x})$. The ϕ^i permit us to characterize those allocations that do not harm any of the N concerned agents. For an allocation $(\mathbf{x}, t^1, \ldots, t^N)$ not to be to the disadvantage any of the N concerned agents, it is necessary and sufficient that

$$U^i(\mathbf{x}, R^i - t^i) \geq U^i(0, R^i), \qquad i = 1, \ldots, N. \tag{1.9}$$

These conditions are equivalent to

$$U^i(\mathbf{x}, R^i - t^i) \geq U^i\{\mathbf{x}, R^i - \phi^i(\mathbf{x})\},$$

and therefore also to

$$t^i \leq \phi^i(\mathbf{x}).$$

In addition, since $\Sigma_{i=1}^{N} t^i = C(\mathbf{x})$, we see that $S(\mathbf{x}) \geq 0$ is a necessary

---

[13] See however section 4 in this chapter.

condition for $(\mathbf{x}, t^1, \ldots, t^N)$ not to be to the disadvantage of any of the N concerned agents. Clearly, it is not sufficient.

The ϕ^i and S allow us to describe, in terms that show off the distributive aspects, the transition from the initial situation I without public goods to a situation that is both efficient and not disadvantageous to any of the N concerned agents, i.e. some point E on the arc $G_1 G_2$ in Figure 1.2. Let $(\mathbf{x}, t^1, \ldots, t^N)$ be the allocation corresponding to such a point. This transition works just as if a two-step decision procedure had been used by a collective authority:

1. The vector $\mathbf{x}$ of public goods is created. At the same time, a contribution equal to $\phi^i(\mathbf{x})$ is collected from each agent i for whom $\phi^i(\mathbf{x}) > 0$, and a compensation equal to $-\phi^i(\mathbf{x})$ is given to each agent i for whom $\phi^i(\mathbf{x}) < 0$. Once this is completed,
    — the utility of each agent has not changed and therefore the distributive consequences of the creation of $\mathbf{x}$ have been neutralized;
    — the collective authority will have available, once $C(\mathbf{x})$ is paid, a surplus equal to $S(\mathbf{x})$.
2. The surplus $S(\mathbf{x})$ is shared between the N agents so that the portion[14] going to i is
    $$\phi^i(\mathbf{x}) - t^i \geqslant 0.$$
    It is certainly a distribution of $S(\mathbf{x})$ since
    $$\sum_{i=1}^{N} \{\phi^i(\mathbf{x}) - t^i\} = \sum_{i=1}^{N} \phi^i(\mathbf{x}) - C(\mathbf{x}) = S(\mathbf{x}).$$
    When this second step is completed,
    — the available income of i is
    $$\{R^i - \phi^i(\mathbf{x})\} + \{\phi^i(\mathbf{x}) - t^i\} = R^i - t^i;$$
    — the utility of i has been increased from the initial level $U^i(0, R^i)$ to the final level $U^i(\mathbf{x}, R^i - t^i)$.

Many cost–benefit analyses recommend the realization of a proposed project on the basis of the prediction of a positive collective surplus. What we have just seen demonstrates two reasons for not

---

[14] Which should not be thought of as an 'income-equivalent' for i, because
$$U^i(0, R^i) = U^i(\mathbf{x}, R^i - \phi^i)$$
does not generally imply that we also have
$$U^i\{0, R^i + (\phi^i - t^i)\} = U^i(\mathbf{x}, R^i - t^i).$$

accepting this approach. First, a realization (in our model, the level **x** of public goods) may offer a collective surplus $S(\mathbf{x})$ that is positive, but nevertheless may be far from efficiency. Second, a positive collective surplus does not ensure that the realization is not disadvantageous to any of the concerned agents. This is not surprising, since the collective surplus alone does not carry any information on the distribution of the advantages and disadvantages. In fact, to depend upon the existence of the collective surplus alone as the basis for a decision creates a bias in favour of those whose initial income is the most high, because $\phi^i(\mathbf{x})$, and, by consequence, i's influence on the choice of the allocation, are increasing in R^i. Will the resulting advantage be counterbalanced by appropriate deductions?

The point $\tilde{E}$ in Figure 1.2 would still be advantageous for the two participants if we take as our point of departure $\bar{F}$ rather than I. This would not be true for $\hat{E}$, which the first participant would rather avoid by adopting the individual technology. If he could block $\hat{E}$ in this way, the only efficient allocations that could be put into effect are those corresponding to the points on the arc $B_1 B_2$ that are located in the north-east quadrant issuing from $\bar{F}$.

The point of reference, I or $\bar{F}$, determines the degree of freedom of the collective authority as far as distributive objectives are concerned. The existence of a private technology, however, does not prevent I from being the point of reference if the collectivity is able to impose the use of the collective technology. In this case $\hat{E}$ could be enacted in spite of $\bar{F}$.

One constantly runs across this problem of property rights, that is of the definition of an initial reference point from which the rights of participants are set. Different countries offer different approaches to the matter, which can be compared using the concepts and methods that have been introduced in this section.

Dutch law, for example, foresees that if, because of the construction of some public infrastructure, 'an individual suffers damages that he cannot reasonably support, the Town Council must accord him a just compensation'. Similarly, the Land Compensation Act voted in 1973 by the British Parliament proposes a general principle of compensation for all physical damages: sound vibrations, odours, fumes resulting from solid or liquid wastes, etc. The introduction of this Act was motivated by considerations of justice, and also of efficiency. Efficiency indeed suffers from the absence of adequate compensation, since this absence incites the promoter of the project to ignore damages whose recognition could have revealed the inefficiency of the project.

In these two countries, the Netherlands and the United Kingdom, public institutions are also given the responsibility to recoup an important part of the increase in value of the land made available for construction, or in other words the land where the existence of public infrastructure allows the construction of housing or office buildings. This means that, in the language of our model, some financial contributions are collected from those who benefit from the public goods. This arrangement is extremely important, for it is frequently better to do nothing than to pay compensations without also collecting contributions. Let us imagine, for example, an area which it would seem socially advantageous to furnish with a public infrastructure permitting urbanization, but under the condition that the development would be concentrated in just one zone of the area, either to reduce costs or to preserve a natural or historical space, or for any other reason. If the increase in land values is not recouped from the owners located in the zone where development is authorized, one can expect the owners located in the rest of the area will demand compensations, completely undeserved in the logic of our model, but whose menace might lead the public authority to accept an urbanization dispersed over the entire area. Such a situation is not exceptional in France, and explains the hostility of the French civil service to any form of indemnification of 'servitudes d'intérêt public', that is of private losses for public gain. It is systematic in the United States, where the 'taking issue' results from the incapacity of the public authorities to limit the development as soon as the limitations affect private property, owing to an interpretation of the Fifth Amendment which improperly favours the property-owners.[15]

The United Kingdom, while having a far more coherent approach to urbanization, still offers a comparable example of incoherence in the management of its rural areas. The collective works for agricultural improvement (drainage, irrigation, and so on) are subsidized with public money by the Department of Agriculture for more than 50 per cent of their cost. If another public institution (such as the Nature Conservancy Council or the Countryside Commission) raises an objection to certain effects of these works—if they lead, for

---

[15] 'Improperly', in the sense of our model. On the 'taking issue', see Bosselman *et al.* (1973).

example, to the conversion to grain crops of lands that should be maintained as humid meadows to retain their ecological or touristic value—it must compensate the landowners and farmers for any financial loss which they might suffer if the public works are cancelled as a result of this objection. Thus, the objecting institution must pay, if such should be the case, the difference between the income derived from grain crops and that derived from cattle breeding, without regard to the fact that part of this difference results from public subsidies. This presents an obvious problem of distributive justice in a country where the majority of landowners, and also the farmers, are in the upper brackets of both wealth and income. There is often a problem of efficiency also, either in the renunciation of land protection as too costly, or in the lack of co-ordination between public institutions, leading one to finance a public good that might no longer be worthwhile while, at the same time, another dissuades a certain number of potential beneficiaries from taking advantage of it.

3. What About 'Free-riders'?

To characterize the efficiency frontier of an economy with public goods is relatively easy, but to obtain the information necessary to reach it from an initial point as I is far more delicate. Then it is necessary to have methods that not only lead to the efficiency frontier, or at least sufficiently near it, but also require a minimum of information-gathering and leave the authority some freedom regarding distribution. Multi-step decision processes have been proposed with these objectives in mind.[16] Such a process starts from a certain allocation. First, a collective authority proposes a modification of the levels of public goods embodied in this allocation and asks for the reactions of the concerned agents in terms of willingness to pay or compensation required. On this basis, and considering the cost of the modification, the authority decides whether or not to actually modify the allocation. If the modification is adopted, the allocation so modified becomes the new point of reference for the following step, which in turn considers further modification. Of course, these

---

[16] For a discussion of the methods and a comparison of several kinds of processes, see Champsaur *et al.* (1977). For a simple illustration, see Henry and Zylberberg (1978).

modifications are not randomly proposed: the method by which they are chosen is crucial from the point of view of fulfilling the desired objectives.

However, are not processes of that kind unrealistic? Let us consider the most simple case, where the decision encompasses only one public good and there is only one level of realization possible. The choice is binary: either the good is produced, or it is not produced (as in the first example in Section 1). In this case the process is reduced to one step, in the course of which the collective authority asks the agents to indicate their ϕ^i (see Section 2 above). But if each agents knows that he will pay in proportion to what he indicates, is he not encouraged to announce an amount smaller than the true ϕ^i, counting on the fact that it will not have much effect on the public decision but will have a favourable effect on his wallet? On the other hand, if he is guaranteed no relation between the response he gives and the contribution he will be asked for later, will he not have a tendency to announce too large an amount?

What are the practical implications of this problem, known as the free-rider problem? It seems possible to keep it under control when the number of agents is not too big. Experiments have shown that free-rider behaviour is relatively rare when each individual's responsibility towards the group is made obvious (see e.g. Bohm 1972, 1984). However, the greater the number of agents involved, the more difficult becomes the accountability.

A recent example deserves attention (see Bohm 1984). In 1982, a Swedish parliamentary commission examined an unusual proposition dealing with management of public finance. That was a year of austerity for the Swedish budget, with each agency attempting to cut all waste. However, the Central Bureau of Statistics, despite a production that was already felt excessive, proposed to provide additional information from the last general census for the use of local governments, permitting them to adjust their policies of urban development. Sweden is divided into 279 local governments whose policy of development has a profound impact, since they determine urban plans—detailed and legally enforceable—and often own much of the developable land, which they rent to builders.

But how could one determine whether this new system of statistics would really be useful for those for whom it was intended? And if it was useful, why provide it free of charge? Naturally, it would not be difficult to make each local government pay for the search and presentation of those data in which it was particularly interested. But first it was necessary to establish the system from the census information and to set it up in such a way that individual consultation would be easy. The system, with its mode of exploitation, would constitute a public good for the 279 local governments. It had a cost which was estimated.[17] Was it worth the price?

To respond to this question, the 279 governments were divided into two categories, each of which was representative of the whole. Each local government was asked to indicate its willingness to pay for the system (the public good) being put into service. In addition, each member of the first category was warned that, if the system were put into effect, it would have to pay an amount equal to its announced willingness to pay; on the other hand, members of the second category were confronted with some fixed amount which they would have to pay in order not to be excluded from the system. This amount was high enough not to look insignificant (the procedure was not to be considered a game), and high enough not to be unfair to the members of the first category; at the same time, it was low enough to exclude access to the public good, if this were actually produced, to the smallest number possible of local governments.

Clearly, members of the first category did not have an incentive to overestimate what they were willing to pay. A lower bound π_1 for the total willingness to pay π of the whole of the 279 local governments can thus be obtained by multiplying the sum of the amounts that members of the first category announced they were willing to pay by the inverse of the proportion of the local governments that they represent.

It is equally clear that members of the second category did not have an incentive to underestimate what they were willing to pay, and, for those whose disposition was at least equal to the fixed amount that they might have to actually pay, there was an incentive to overestimate. This second category thus provides an upper bound π_2 of π.

One can conclude that, if π_1 is not inferior to the cost of production C, then the efficient decision is surely to produce the public good, and if π_2 is not superior to C, the efficient decision is to not produce it. In these two cases the effects of biased announcements would be neutralized. Drawing a conclusion is difficult if π_1 and π_2

---

[17] This is a 0–1 decision; a single version of the system was proposed.

surround C. If π_1 and π_2 are not too far apart, this difficulty does not occur too often. In the Swedish case, it appears that π_1 is greater than C and that the difference $\pi_2 - \pi_1$ amounts to less than 8 per cent of π_1. This latter result is the interesting one for us here, because it shows how limited the free-rider problem has been in this case. Although it is not possible to draw general conclusions at this stage, it is worth stressing that the behaviour of the Swedish local governments confirms the results obtained in previous smaller-scale experiments.

When the problem of free-riding becomes a real threat, one can conceive of ways to thwart its effect. The logic of these methods can be demonstrated in the following example.[18] Assume there is a public good at stake whose technical constraints allow a choice only of 0 or 1. Its production cost is C. The project will affect N economic agents. Let ϕ^i, with $i = 1, \ldots, N$, be the maximum amount that agent i would be willing to pay for the project. Let δ^i be the amount that agent i announces as the maximum that he would be willing to pay for the project.[19]

Each agent, say agent $i = 1$, is invited to participate in the following process, which a collective authorithy organizes. A first set of possible situations by which agent i might be confronted is defined by

$$\sum_{j=2}^{N} \delta^j \geqslant \frac{N-1}{N} C. \qquad (1.10)$$

This translates the fact that the agents other than i are willing to pay more than their share of the public project. Given these conditions, the following rule is applied:

(a) If δ^1 is such that

$$\sum_{i=1}^{N} \delta^i \geqslant C, \qquad (1.11)$$

then the public good is produced and no contribution is asked of 1 (nor does he receive any payment).

[18] For a much more extensive treatment, see Green and Laffont (1979).

[19] In all that follows in this section, we use the abbreviated notation ϕ^i for $\phi^i(1)$. On the other hand, we make the hypothesis that, for each agent i, C/N represents a small enough proportion of his income R^i that the contribution ϕ^i is not modified by a change in R^i smaller than or equal to C/N.

up to now, the personalized prices actually only permit an artificial decentralization. In reinterpreting and somewhat generalizing the model, we shall see that this is not always so, and that personalized prices can lead to a true decentralization, leading to significant reduction in the quantity of information needed regarding the preferences of the N users.

Let us consider a system capable of producing services (generating electricity, transporting people and goods, etc.) in quantity X during each of T periods; these are designated as $i = 1, \ldots, T$. X is the capacity of the system.

What happens during period i? The services produced by the system are consumed by N^i users; these users are designated as (i, j), with $j = 1, \ldots, N^i$. This usage is private; hence the quantities x_j^i consumed respectively by the N^i consumers (i, j) add up to a total quantity that cannot exceed X:

$$\sum_{j=1}^{N^i} x_j^i \leqslant X. \tag{1.31}$$

This division of X in x_j^i is achieved by presenting the N^i users with a price p^i. The x_j^i are thus the individual demands at price p^i:

$$x_j^i = d_j^i(p^i, R_j^i; \ldots), \quad j = 1, \ldots, N^i. \tag{1.32}$$

The suspension points indicate a possible dependence on prices and initial incomes in other periods; for example, user (i', j') in period i' and user (i'', j'') in period i'', might be the same economic agent, present at periods i' and i'' and interested in the services offered in both these periods. By inverting each demand function (1.32), we obtain the equality of the price p^i to the willingness to pay for a marginal increase in x_j^i:

$$\pi_j^i(x_j^i, R_j^i - p^i x_j^i; \ldots) = p^i. \tag{1.33}$$

Condition (1.33) applies to each of the N^i users (i, j) as the x_j^i are their respective demands for the same private good offered at the same price p^i. The total demand for the period i is

$$x^i = \sum_{j=1}^{N^i} d_j^i,$$

and we can rewrite (1.31) as

$$x^i \leqslant X. \tag{1.31'}$$

Up to now, we have only considered the use of the system period by period. Since it is the same system during the T periods, in the sense that X cannot be modulated between periods (as attested by the inequalities (1.31)), X and p^i ($i = 1, \ldots, T$) must be chosen efficiently with reference to this interdependence between periods. The conditions (1.33) imply that each of the N^i users (i, j) is willing to pay the same amount for a marginal increase in X to become available to him in period i, in addition to x_j^i. For this reason, we can analyse the interdependence between periods by considering as a representative for each period, $i = 1, \ldots, T$, just one of the users (i, j), for example $(i, 1)$. For these T users $(i, 1)$, the system is a public good: the same increase in its capacity can be used simultaneously by all. Consequently, as for the quantity produced of any public good, the capacity X can be efficient only if the Samuelson condition is fulfilled, here under the form

$$\sum_{i=1}^{T} \pi_1^i(x_1^i, R_1^i - p^i x_1^i; \ldots) = c, \tag{1.34}$$

or

$$\sum_{i=1}^{T} p^i = c. \tag{1.35}$$

In addition, efficiency requires that conditions (1.31') be supplemented with

$$x^i < X \Rightarrow p^i = 0. \tag{1.36}$$

Indeed, if $x^i < X$ and $p^i > 0$, the way the system is used would not be efficient: that $\pi_j^i > 0$ means that (i, j) would like to increase its consumption, and this would be possible at no cost since the capacity $X - x^i$ would be unused. Conditions (1.31') and (1.36), along with (1.35), constitute a system of $T + 1$ equations in X and p^i ($i = 1, \ldots, T$). As for the $2 \Sigma_{i=1}^{T} N^i$ individual consumptions x_j^i and contributions $t_j^i = p^i x_j^i$, they are determined by the users themselves from (1.32).

Thus, personalized prices, one at each period, allow us to avoid the collection of huge amounts of information that would be necessitated by a direct division of quantities, centrally administered for each period. They are all the more convenient that T is small compared with the N^i, and that information on the aggregate demand in each period is easier to collect. They present the inconvenience of not allowing any freedom of action in distributive matters. This can in part be corrected by using nonlinear prices, but then the information required increases.

Since 1973, opening a railroad tunnel under the English Channel —using shuttles for motor cars and lorries—could have been profitable for a private firm, if only it had considered the application of personalized prices in the sense that we have introduced them in this section. One firm was actually interested enough in the project to commision a serious and detailed study of the estimated costs and demand. The study settled on the conclusion that the profits of the firm managing the Tunnel would be maximized if:

— the terminals giving access to the Tunnel had a capacity of 2,050 vehicles per hour, the vehicle of reference being a private motor car of average size;
— there were a price of £19 (1973 value) for a one-way trip of a vehicle of reference.

Under these conditions, the gross annual profit, before amortization for the Tunnel itself, would be £23 million. This profit was insufficient for paying off the Tunnel.

S. Glaister (1976) noticed, some time after this study had appeared, that its conclusion is tied to a conceptual error. An infrastructure like the Tunnel and its terminals is a public good for the users who use it at different periods of the year as well as different hours of the same day. To these users should be offered personalized prices, varying according to the time and date of use. Having reworked the study, Glaister reached the conclusion that the profits of the firm managing the Tunnel would be maximized if:

— the terminals giving access to the Tunnel had a capacity of 520 vehicles per hour:
— there were a price schedule distinguishing seventeen rate periods in the year, and thus a range of £16–£56 for a one-way trip of a vehicle of reference.

Under these conditions, the gross annual profit before amortization for the tunnel would be £47 million, more than required for paying off the Tunnel.

2
Polluter-Pays and Other Principles: Alleviating External Effects

1. 'The Polluters Shall Be the Payers'

In 1972 the member countries of the Organization for Economic Co-operation and Development (OECD) adopted, as advised by the organization, the 'Polluter-Pays Principle' (PPP). According to this principle,

Public measures are . . . necessary to reduce pollution and to reach a better allocation of resources by ensuring that prices of goods depending on the quality and/or quantity of environmental resources reflect more closely their relative scarcity and that economic agents concerned react accordingly. . . . The Principle means that the polluter should bear the expenses of carrying out the above mentioned measures decided by public authorities to ensure that the environment is in an acceptable state. In other words, the cost of these measures should be reflected in the cost of the goods and services which cause pollution in production and/or consumption.[1]

The management of water resources provides a most appropriate arena in which to examine the implementation of these intentions.[2] Water authorities like the French Agences de Bassin, the Dutch Waterschappen, and the West German Genossenschaften are trying to put them into practice. A simple model will show on what basis and with what effect this is occurring.

Around a lake reside N inhabitants who want the water to be of the best possible quality. Here, we also find M factories who would like to pour wastes into the lake, with a minimum of restrictions; these diminish the quality of the water. Let $\bar{x}$ be the water quality when no factories have emptied wastes into the water. When the

---

[1] OECD (1975).
[2] Experiments in management of air quality also merit examination; see the end of this section.

(b) If δ^1 is such that

$$\sum_{i=1}^{N} \delta^i < C, \tag{1.12}$$

then the public good is not produced and agent 1[20] is given a payment equal to

$$C - \sum_{j=2}^{n} \delta^j. \tag{1.13}$$

Using the above rule in any situation where (1.10) is satisfied ensures that 1 will not have any incentive to announce $\delta^1 \neq \phi^1$, in other words to not tell the truth. Indeed:

(a) If ϕ^1 is such that

$$\phi^1 + \sum_{j=2}^{N} \delta^j \geqslant C, \tag{1.14}$$

in other words, if the true contribution of 1 in addition to the announced contributions of the $N-1$ other participants assures the financing of the public good, then the only lie that would have a result different from the truth is one that would reverse the inequality (1.14) so that

$$\delta^1 + \sum_{j=2}^{N} \delta^j < C. \tag{1.15}$$

In this case, 1 would receive $C - \Sigma_{j=2}^{N} \delta^j$ which, owing to (1.14), would be inferior to the minimum amount that would compensate for the absence of the public good.

(b) If ϕ^1 is such that

$$\phi^1 + \sum_{j=2}^{N} \delta^j < C, \tag{1.16}$$

in other words, if the true contribution of 1 in addition to the announced contributions of the $N-1$ other participants does not assure the financing of the public good, then the only lie that would have a result different from the truth is one that would reverse the inequality (1.16) so that

$$\delta^1 + \sum_{j=2}^{N} \delta^j \geqslant C. \tag{1.17}$$

In this case, 1 would not receive $C - \Sigma_{j=2}^{N} \delta^j$ which, owing to (1.16), is more than what the public good is worth to him.

---

[20] Agent 1 is in this case called a pivotal agent.

The second set of possible situations, complementary to the first one from the point of view of agent 1, is defined by

$$\sum_{j=2}^{N} \delta^j < \frac{N-1}{N} C. \tag{1.18}$$

Given these conditions, the following rule is applied:

(a) If δ^1 is such that

$$\sum_{i=1}^{N} \delta^i < C, \tag{1.19}$$

then the public good is not produced. No financial contribution is asked of 1, and he receives no payment.

(b) If δ^1 is such that

$$\sum_{i=1}^{N} \delta^i \geqslant C, \tag{1.20}$$

then the public good is produced. Agent 1[21] must pay a financial contribution equal to

$$C - \sum_{j=2}^{N} \delta^j. \tag{1.21}$$

We can see that, in any situation with (1.18) satisfied, the application of the above rule again prompts agent 1 to announce his true willingness to pay.

It appears that the collective authority will produce (resp. not produce) the public good if $\Sigma_{i=1}^{N} \phi^i$ is superior (resp. inferior) to C, i.e. when appropriate. In addition, no agent i is put into a situation of having to pay a contribution superior to ϕ^i (resp. 0) if the public good is (resp. is not) produced.

However, in addition to the fact that budget balance is not assured by this mechanism, there are problems in terms of distribution. Let us imagine, for example, that N is even and that the population of agents interested in the realization of the public good is constituted of two categories, each made up of $N/2$ identical agents. Consider a case where, for the first category, ϕ^1 is equal to $1.9(C/N)$ and, for the second category, ϕ^2 is equal to $0.1\,\phi^1$. In view of the previously stated rules, the public good is produced. Further, if N is greater than or equal to 20, no contribution is asked of anyone, which is clearly far more to the advantage of the first category than the second.

It is possible in theory, by using elaborated decision-making processes, to achieve budget balance and to control to a certain

---

[21] Agent 1 is again in this case a pivotal agent.

extent the distributive consequences of an allocation of public goods, while at the same time using a system of incentives to induce a revelation of the true willingness to pay for the allocation (see Laffont and Maskin 1982). But this is certainly not possible in practice when the number of agents is large. A more practical response is considered in Section 4 below, and later on in Chapter 3.

4. Personalized Prices and Peak Pricing

With a limited number of participants—such as the Swedish local governments or the representatives of the inhabitants of a middle-sized town—it is possible to set the individual contributions in conformation with a previously fixed distributive policy. When the users of the public good are more numerous and more hetero-geneous, it is no longer possible to control things so carefully. One must inevitably turn to procedures that are more automatic, less demanding in exchange of information, and more difficult to contest. This is exactly what EDF (Electricité de France), the French national electricity company, does with its customers, and it is what Euro-tunnel will do with those who travel under the English Channel.

How do we go about introducing some automatism and reducing the requirements for information? Let us consider an efficient allo-cation $(x, t^1, \ldots, t^N)$;[22] being efficient, it satisfies the Samuelson condition,

$$\sum_{i=1}^{N} \pi^i(x, R^i - t^i) = c. \tag{1.22}$$

We are now going to constrain it further by imposing the N conditions $(i = 1, \ldots, N)$

$$t^i = \pi^i(x, R^i - t^i)x. \tag{1.23}$$

These conditions can also be written

$$t^i = p^i x \tag{1.24}$$

if we define p^i as the marginal rate of substitution $\pi^i(x, R^i - t^i)$, i.e. if

$$p^i = \pi^i(x, R^i - t^i). \tag{1.25}$$

---

[22] We treat the question of personalized prices in the case of a single public good—to lighten the notation—and with constant returns, i.e. with $C(x) = cx$. This second restriction simplifies the treatment by avoiding the problem of the distribution of the profit realized by the enterprise producing the public good. This problem is dealt with in Milleron (1972).

Consider an efficient allocation[23] $(x_L, t_L^1, \ldots, t_L^N)$, which also satisfies the conditions (1.23). Because of (1.23) and (1.24), an equivalent characterization for this allocation is $(x_L, p_L^1, \ldots, p_L^N)$, with $p_L^i = \pi^i(x_L, R^i - t_L^i)$; it satisfies the conditions

$$\sum_{i=1}^{N} p^i = c \tag{1.22'}$$

and, for $i = 1, \ldots, N$,

$$p^i = \pi^i(x, R^i - p^i x) \tag{1.23'}$$

which we obtain by substituting the p^i for the t^i in (1.22) and (1.23).

From an accounting perspective, we can read (1.24) in the following way: i buys x_L at the price p_L^i, or, more precisely, the financial contribution t^i paid by i is calculated on the basis of a personalized price p_L^i. But is p_L^i a price in a more operational sense? Is it a signal conveying information to i and directing his consumption choices?

Let us imagine making i the following proposition: you may use as much of the good as you desire as long as you pay for it at the price p_L^i. We thus present the good to i as if it were a private good, and i reacts as he would with a private good: he chooses his demand x^i in such a way as to maximize his utility subject to the budget constraint

$$p_L^i x^i + y^i = R^i. \tag{1.26}$$

He thus chooses x^i to equalize

$$\frac{\partial U^i / \partial x^i}{\partial U^i / \partial y^i} = p_L^i, \tag{1.27}$$

i.e.

$$\pi^i(x^i, y^i) = p_L^i. \tag{1.28}$$

Taking (1.26) into consideration, we can rewrite (1.28) in the form

$$\pi^i(x^i, R^i - p_L^i x^i) = p_L^i, \tag{1.29}$$

which is simply (1.23'). Choosing

$$x^i = x_L \tag{1.30}$$

thus maximizes i's utility subject to his budget constraint.

What interest can there be in decentralizing the choices through personalized prices p^i rather than by announcing x and the respective t^i to the N users? After all, to be able to decentralize, we must first calculate x and the t^i. In the model with which we have been working

---

[23] Such an allocation is called a Lindahl equilibrium, named after the Swedish economist who was the first to appreciate its significance.

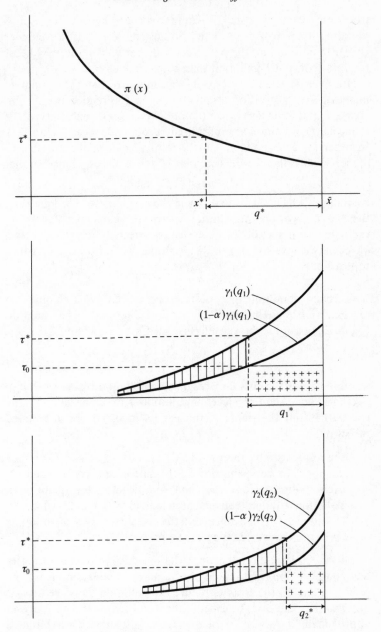

Fig. 2.1

tive; being equal to $\gamma_j(q_j^*)$, it would incite j to choose the level of pollution q_j^*. For $q_j > q_j^*$, it would cost more to pay the effluent charge than to reduce the pollution, while for $q_j < q_j^*$, it would cost more to reduce the pollution than to pay the charge.

However, it is not exactly in this manner that the system of financing and motivation usually functions. In practice, the effluent charge τ_0 put into effect is less than τ^*. At the same time, the costs of reducing the pollution are subsidized at some rate α (see Figure 2.1). In order for each polluter j to be motivated to make an efficient choice, it must then be the case that τ_0 and α be determined so that

$$(1 - \alpha)\gamma_j(q_j^*) = \tau_0, \tag{2.6}$$

a condition which means that it is in the best interest of j, equalizing the charge τ_0 per unit of pollution and the marginal cost of reducing the pollution it actually bears, to choose precisely the efficient level q_j^*. Since we have, for all j, $\gamma_j(q_j^*) = \tau^*$, the N conditions (2.6) reduce to just one:

$$(1 - \alpha)\tau^* = \tau_0. \tag{2.7}$$

A second condition may be imposed on τ_0 and α so that the revenue from the effluent charges collected (cross-hatched area on Figure 2.1) pays for the subsidies (shaded area on Figure 2.1):

$$\tau_0 \sum_{j=1}^{M} q_j^* = \alpha \sum_{j=1}^{M} \Gamma_j(q_j^*) \tag{2.8}$$

where $\Gamma_j(q_j^*)$ is the cost for j to limit its pollution to the level q_j^*.

Under this system, the level of pollution is the same as under the strict PPP, but the rights of the parties involved are distributed rather differently:

— the residents have the right to the quality x^* of the water; they cannot claim compensation for the difference between $\bar{x}$ and x^*;
— every polluter j has the right to discharge the quantity of pollution q_j it finds convenient in light of both the marginal cost $(1 - \alpha)\gamma_j(q_j)$ of reducing q_j and the marginal cost τ_0 of polluting; these are the marginal costs as j perceives them.

All that precedes assumes that the responsible public authority has complete information on the damages that result from the pollution and on the costs to reduce the pollution. However, this is not generally the case. In general, the public authority has only an approximate knowledge of the damage π, and an even more limited knowledge of the marginal cost functions γ_j. Is the authority then in a position to incite the polluters to choose the efficient levels of pollution q_j^*, even if it is no longer capable of calculating them? We are going to show how an almost positive response may be given to this question by adapting our model to situations where the public authority has only a small amount of information. The model thus adapted formalizes and extends experiments in transactions of rights to pollute the air which were conducted in the United States, primarily in California.

In the introduction to a report dealing with American, mainly Californian, experiments of transactions in air pollution rights, the US General Accounting Office[5] writes:

The traditional[6] air pollution control system, commonly known as command and control, is characterized by rules dictating specific methods of pollution abatement and limits on the amounts of pollution from each industrial plant and even from each source of pollution within a plant. By contrast, a market approach to air pollution control would allow firms considerable flexibility in choosing ways to meet the air quality mandate of the Clean Air Act. For instance, a steel firm might find it cheaper to pay chemical companies to control their air pollution, rather than control that same amount of pollution itself. GAO's review of a number of studies suggests that a full-scale market in air pollution entitlements could, in some instances, save industry as much as 90% in pollution abatement costs as compared to command and control.

This kind of market could not be started and then function on the desired scale without the intervention of some organizer. This has already been demonstrated in the San Francisco Bay Area experience: 'The basic element for developing a market in air pollution entitlements are present in the San Franscisco Bay Area. An emissions reduction bank, where suppliers of air pollution entitlements receive credit for pollution curtailments not legally required, offers opportunities to reduce transaction costs in future trading.'

It is clear that a public authority charged to set individual quotas cannot know with a sufficient precision, at a given moment, the conditions of production of each polluter, to say nothing of their changes over time. Hence a regulatory device that would operate without such detailed information and still perform satisfactorily in terms of quality and costs would be welcome. As we shall see, such a

[5] GAO (1982).
[6] The PPP has not yet had many applications in the USA; instead, complicated systems of quotas and ceilings have been devised.

device can be implemented when the public authority in charge can measure or estimate the marginal damage π for a sufficient number of possible levels of pollution.[7] About the marginal costs γ_j, the authority has only the following information: they are continuous and decreasing functions of the corresponding q_j. In spite of not knowing the optimal level q^* of pollution, the authority is able to estimate a lower and an upper bound:

$$z_1 < q^* < z_K.$$

The less information the authority has, the farther apart will be the two bounds z_1 and z_K.

Despite the small amount of information the public authority so possesses, it can nevertheless formulate a rule having the following effects: (1) the level of pollution resulting from the application of the rule is not far from q^*, i.e. from the optimal level that remains unknown; (2) the division between the M polluters of this resulting level is efficient.

We first consider the case where the polluters do not start with any right to pollute. To formulate the rule, let us subdivide the interval $[z_1, z_K]$ into $K - 1$ intervals $[z_k, z_{k+1}]$. The extremities of these intervals are the levels of pollution at which the public authority knows the corresponding marginal damages $\pi(x_k)$, with $x_k = \bar{x} - z_k$. We also use the notation, for $k = 1, \ldots, K$,

$$\tau_k = \pi(x_k) \quad \text{and} \quad \tau^* = \pi(x^*);$$

whereas the τ_k are known, τ^* is obviously not known. Under these circumstances, the public authority formulates the following rule:

(a) Each polluter must be in possession of a number of rights to pollute equal to the pollution that it discharges. The rights are bought from the public authority.

(b) The authority announces it is ready to sell rights to pollute at a price that is at least τ_1[8] if the total number z of rights sold is at most z_1; and at a price that is at least τ_2 if the total number z of rights sold is greater than z_1 and is at most z_2; and so on, i.e. at a price that is at least τ_{k+1} if $z_k < z \leqslant z_{k+1}$ ($k = 1, \ldots, K - 1$). The maximum number of rights offered is z_K.

---

[7] Here also we ignore income effects.

[8] More explicitly, if the number z of rights sold is strictly smaller than z_1, then the price is τ_1; if $z_1 < z < z_2$, the price is τ_2; however, if z is exactly equal to z_1, the price is in the interval $[\tau_1, \tau_2]$, and determined in such a way that the demand is exactly equal to z_1.

The supply $z(\tau)$ so announced by the authority is represented by the step function in Figures 2.2 and 2.3. This function is determined, from the marginal damage π, by the way in which the interval $[z_1, z_K]$ is partitioned; it is an approximation of π. It will be no surprise that such an approximation to the damage function as a supply function for rights to pollute works better the smaller the intervals $[z_k, z_{k+1}]$.

Within this framework, an equilibrium price in the market for rights to pollute is a price τ^e such that:

1. at the price τ^e, the demand[9] does not exceed the maximum supply,
$$q(\tau^e) \leqslant z(\tau^e);$$

2. at any price σ less that τ^e, the demand exceeds the supply,
$$\forall \sigma < \tau^e, \quad q(\sigma) > z(\sigma).$$

From the properties of the functions π and γ_j, it is clear that an equilibrium price τ^e exists and is unique.

There exists, of course, a k such that

$$z_k \leqslant q^* \leqslant z_{k+1}. \tag{2.9}$$

Even though this k is unknown, as is q^*, we can show that the demand $q(\tau^e)$ at the equilibrium price is close to q^*, in the sense that

$$z_k \leqslant q(\tau^e) \leqslant z_{k+1}, \tag{2.10}$$

i.e. the distance between $q(\tau^e)$ and q^* is at most the distance between z_k and z_{k+1}.[10] Moreover, the distribution of $q(\tau^e)$ among the polluters is clearly efficient, as the choice of $q_j(\tau^e)$ is made by every polluter j according to the same price τ^e so that (2.2) is satisfied. Hence the social loss resulting from the implementation of $q(\tau^e)$ instead of q^* can be made as small as desired, provided z_k is close enough to z_{k+1} for all k ($k = 1, \ldots, K-1$); the latter condition must be fulfilled for all k because the authority does not know beforehand which k satisfies $z_k \leqslant q^* \leqslant z_{k+1}$.

These results provide a rigorous basis for regulating external effects by auctioning rights. However, the preceding argument ignores the possibility that the polluters might own rights to pollute before the auctioning process begins; this is in fact no restriction. If

---

[9] The total demand $q(\tau)$ is the sum of the individual demands $q_j(\tau)$ ($j = 1, \ldots, M$) determined by the conditions $\gamma_j(q_j) = \tau$. These functions of τ are continuous and decreasing.

[10] This is proved at the end of the present section.

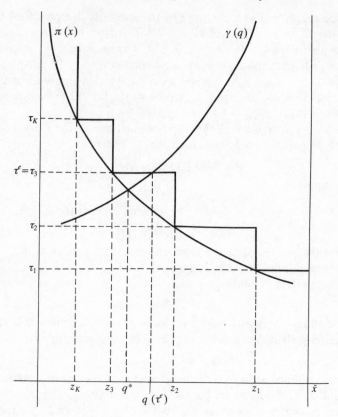

$$\text{Fig. 2.2}$$

the polluters do possess such rights, the public authority may indeed reformulate the rule in the following way:[11]

(a) It could remain unchanged.
(b) Any owner of rights is free to sell any number of them to anyone interested in buying them, at a price that suits both parties.
(c) When $\phi \leqslant z_K$, the authority announces it is ready both to buy rights (z' designates the total number of rights purchased), at a

---

[11] We shall write ϕ for the total number of rights held initially by the polluters (or other agents), and m for the integer between 0 and K such that $z_m < \phi \leqslant z_{m+1}$, with $z_0 = 0$ and $z_{K+1} = +\infty$.

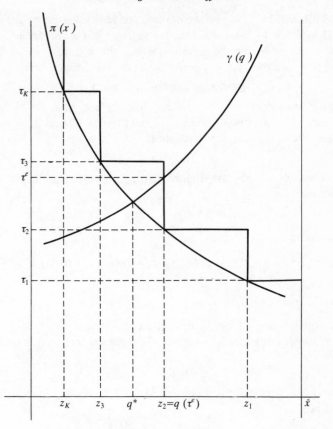

FIG. 2.3

price τ which is at most

$$\tau_{k+1} \quad \text{if} \quad z_k < \phi - z' \leqslant z_{k+1}, \quad k = 0, \dots, m,$$

and to sell rights (z'' designates the total number of rights sold), at a price τ which is at least

$$\tau_{k+1} \quad \text{if} \quad z_k < \phi + z'' \leqslant z_{k+1}, \quad k = m, \dots, K-1.$$

When $\phi \geqslant z_K$, the authority can only buy. With this rule, the market functions in such a way that the previous results still hold: the market equilibrium provides an approximation which is still the more accurate the better the information about π held by the public authority.

As stated earlier, we now complete this section by proving that q^* and $q(\tau^e)$ lie in the same interval $[z_k, z_{k+1}]$. For notational simplicity, we consider the situation where the polluters do not own rights before the market opens. We shall prove that

$$z_k \leqslant q^* \leqslant z_{k+1} \text{ implies } z_k \leqslant q(\tau^e) \leqslant z_{k+1}.$$

There are two cases to consider: $q(\tau_{k+1}) \geqslant z_k$ and $q(\tau_{k+1}) < z_k$. These cases correspond respectively to Figures 2.2 and 2.3. In both cases, use is made of the inequalities

$$q(\tau_k) \geqslant q^* \geqslant q(\tau_{k+1}).$$

When $q(\tau_{k+1}) \geqslant z_k$ (see Figure 2.2), τ_{k+1} is the equilibrium price because

1. $$q(\tau_{k+1}) \leqslant q^* \leqslant z_{k+1} \quad \text{and} \quad z_{k+1} = z(\tau_{k+1})$$

and, at any $\sigma < \tau_{k+1}$,

2. $$q(\sigma) > q(\tau_{k+1}) \geqslant z_k \quad \text{and} \quad z_k \geqslant z(\sigma).$$

As it is clear that

$$z_k \leqslant q(\tau_{k+1}) \leqslant z_{k+1},$$

the result is proved for the first case considered.

When $q(\tau_{k+1}) < z_k$ (see Figure 2.3), there exists a unique price τ^e such that

$$q(\tau^e) = z_k \quad \text{with} \quad \tau_{k+1} > \tau^e \geqslant \tau_k.$$

This holds because q is a continuous and decreasing function of τ and because

$$q(\tau_{k+1}) < z_k \leqslant q(\tau_k).$$

From the equality $q(\tau^e) = z(\tau^e)$, it is clear that τ^e is the equilibrium price. As $q(\tau^e) = z_k$, the result is proved for the second case as well.

2. Public Goods Subject to Crowding

Consider a public facility, for example a motorway. The quality of the service offered by that facility varies; for instance, the ease of circulation on the motorway will be affected by the traffic flow. This quality is then a function $x(Q, C)$ of

— the size of the facility, hence the cost C of its construction: the higher C, the larger the facility, and the higher the quality of the service; x is thus an increasing function of C;

— the load Q on the facility: the heavier the load, the lower the quality of the service; x is thus a decreasing function of Q.

The load Q is itself an increasing function $Q = H(q^1, \ldots, q^N)$ of the intensity q^i with which each agent i uses the facility. In our example, Q is the crowding of the motorway to which each user contributes through his presence on the road, his style of driving, the characteristics of his vehicle, etc., i.e. through a parameter q^i which is his own and which he determines himself.

Under these conditions, agent i can be seen as consuming a quantity x of a public good, a quantity q^i of a private good, the consumption of which is linked to the public good, and a quantity y^i of a composite private good playing the same role of numeraire as in Section 2 of Chapter 1. This quantity y^i is obtained by subtracting from the initial income R^i the contribution t^i of i to the financing of the public good as well as the cost $c^i(q^i)$ paid by i when he consumes q^i:

$$y^i = R^i - t^i - c^i(q^i).$$

In the example of the highway, $c^i(q^i)$ is the cost of the petrol, plus the depreciation of the vehicle, etc.[12] Let $U^i(x, q^i, y^i)$ be i's utility function.

The problem of pollution of a lake examined in Section 1 of this chapter is another illustration—a simple one—of a public good subject to crowding. Indeed, in this case,

$$H(q^1, \ldots, q^N) = \sum_{i=1}^{N} q^i$$

$$x(Q, C) = \bar{x} - Q$$

$$C = 0 \quad \text{and} \quad c^i = 0 \quad (i = 1, \ldots, N).$$

Here, there are two categories of agents concerned by the pollution, with fundamentally different preferences: for a resident there is no consumption q^i, and, on the other hand, no polluter cares about x.

In the same way that we established the Samuelson conditions in Section 2 of Chapter 1 let us now search for the necessary conditions

---

[12] The more kilometres travelled by the vehicle and the larger it is, the more petrol it consumes. It is this sort of dependence that is represented by $c^i(q^i)$. But the consumption increases also with crowding. This second type of dependence is recorded through U^i as a function of x and x a function of Q. We find in Glaister (1981), besides a particularly clear exposition of the fundamentals of transportation economics, the empirical data for these two types of dependence.

for efficiency when there is a public good subject to crowding. In this case, we must maximize

$$U^1\{x(Q, C), q^1, R^1 - t^1 - c^1(q^1)\}, \tag{2.11}$$

subject to the constraints

$$U^j\{x(Q, C), q^j, R^j - t^j - c^j(q^j)\} = u^j, \quad j = 2, \ldots, N, \tag{2.12}$$

$$\sum_{i=1}^{N} t^i - C = 0, \tag{2.13}$$

and

$$-H(q^1, \ldots, q^N) + Q = 0. \tag{2.14}$$

The $N - 1$ first constraints fix at predetermined levels u^j the utilities of all agents other than agent 1, whose utility we maximize. Condition (2.13) says that the cost of the centralized production of the public good, that is the production of x from C, is covered exactly by the contributions t^i. The last condition indicates how the individual q^i interact to generate the load Q; each agent contributes relatively more to the decentralized production of the public good as his q^i is relatively smaller.

Designating by μ^j ($j = 2, \ldots, N$), λ, and σ the multipliers associated with the constraints (2.12), (2.13), and (2.14), we have the Lagrangean

$$\mathcal{L} = U^1\{x(Q, C), q^1, R^1 - t^1 - c^1(q^1)\}$$

$$+ \sum_{j=2}^{N} \mu^j U^j\{x(Q, C), q^j, R^j - t^j - c^j(q^j)\}$$

$$+ \lambda\left(\sum_{i=1}^{N} t^i - C\right) + \sigma\{-H(q^1, \ldots, q^N) + Q\}.$$

By setting the derivatives of the Lagrangean, with respect to C, t^i, q^i ($i = 1, \ldots, N$), and Q, equal to zero, we obtain the first-order necessary conditions for the constrained maximization of U^1:

$$\frac{\partial \mathcal{L}}{\partial C} = \frac{\partial U^1}{\partial x}\frac{\partial x}{\partial C} + \sum_{j=2}^{N} \mu^j \frac{\partial U^j}{\partial x}\frac{\partial x}{\partial C} - \lambda = 0$$

$$\frac{\partial \mathcal{L}}{\partial t^1} = -\frac{\partial U^1}{\partial y^1} + \lambda = 0$$

$$\frac{\partial \mathcal{L}}{\partial t^j} = -\mu^j \frac{\partial U^j}{\partial y^j} + \lambda = 0, \ j = 2, \ldots, N$$

$$\frac{\partial \mathcal{L}}{\partial q^1} = \frac{\partial U^1}{\partial q^1} - \frac{\partial U^1}{\partial y^1}\frac{dc^1}{dq^1} - \sigma \frac{\partial H}{\partial q^1} = 0$$

$$\frac{\partial \mathscr{L}}{\partial q^j} = \mu^j \left(\frac{\partial U^j}{\partial q^j} - \frac{\partial U^j}{\partial y^j} \frac{dc^j}{dq^j} \right) - \sigma \frac{\partial H}{\partial q^j} = 0, \quad j = 2, \ldots, N$$

$$\frac{\partial \mathscr{L}}{\partial Q} = \frac{\partial U^1}{\partial x} \frac{\partial x}{\partial Q} + \sum_{j=2}^{N} \mu^j \frac{\partial U^j}{\partial x} \frac{\partial x}{\partial Q} + \sigma = 0.$$

To interpret these conditions more easily, after eliminating the μ^j, we rewrite them in the following form:

$$\sum_{i=1}^{N} \pi^i(x, y^i) = \left(\frac{\partial x}{\partial C} \right)^{-1} \tag{2.15}$$

$$\pi^i(q^i, y^i) = \frac{dc^i}{dq^i} + \frac{\sigma}{\lambda} \frac{\partial H}{\partial q^i}, \quad i = 1, \ldots, N \tag{2.16}$$

$$\sum_{i=1}^{N} \pi^i(x, y^i) = -\frac{\sigma}{\lambda} \left(\frac{\partial x}{\partial Q} \right)^{-1} \tag{2.17}$$

If we hold Q constant in the function $x(Q, C)$, there remains a function x increasing in C, whose inverse function is the cost of the centralized production of x with Q fixed. The derivative of this cost with respect to x being, under these conditions, the algebraic inverse of $\partial x/\partial C$, we see that condition (2.15) is the immediate generalization of the Samuelson condition (i.e. (1.7) of Chapter 1). Condition (2.17) is also Samuelson's condition, relative this time to the decentralized production of the public good. It generalizes condition (2.3) in this chapter. Condition (2.17) allows us to interpret the ratio σ/λ as the collective willingness to pay for $-(\partial x/\partial Q)$, i.e. for the increase in x that results from a marginal decrease in Q. Thus, the conditions (2.16), which generalize (2.2), are interpreted simply for each agent i as the equality between, on the one hand, the marginal rate of substitution of the numeraire y^i for the private good q^i and, on the other hand, the marginal cost of q^i. This marginal cost is the sum of the marginal cost dc^i/dq^i directly supported by i and the marginal cost $(\sigma/\lambda)(\partial H/\partial q^i)$ imposed by i on the whole set of the N concerned agents (external effect). This $(\sigma/\lambda)(\partial H/\partial q^i)$ is indeed the collective loss that is due to the decrease in x which results, through the increase $\partial H/\partial q^i$ in Q, from a marginal increase in q^i. When he chooses his consumption q^i, agent i is naturally sensitive only to that component of the marginal cost that he pays directly, i.e. dc^i/dq^i. One way to make him also sensitive to $(\sigma/\lambda)(\partial H/\partial q^i)$, the other component of the marginal cost, would be to impose on him the payment of a toll[13] $\tau_i^* q^i$, of which the rate is precisely

$$\tau_i^* = \frac{\sigma}{\lambda} \frac{\partial H}{\partial q^i}.$$

In the case of the polluters around the lake, all of the q^i have the same effect on Q, hence all the τ_i^* are equal to the same τ^*.

It is easily seen that σ/λ is also the increase in C that exactly compensates the effect on x of a marginal increase in Q; keeping x constant, we indeed have

$$\frac{dC}{dQ} = \frac{\sigma}{\lambda}. \tag{2.18}$$

This is because, from $x(C, Q) = k$, and k a constant, we get

$$\frac{\partial x}{\partial C} dC + \frac{\partial x}{\partial Q} dQ = 0;$$

in other words,

$$\frac{dC}{dQ} = -\frac{\partial x}{\partial Q} \left(\frac{\partial x}{\partial C} \right)^{-1}. \tag{2.19}$$

Condition (2.18) means that the increase in C, which neutralizes the effect on x of a marginal increase in Q, is σ/λ; this is also, as we see from (2.16), the marginal opportunity cost of refraining (as an alternative way to keep x constant) from increasing Q.

To show the link between the approach to public goods which has been exposed here and another approach, known as the theory of clubs or of local public goods, let us consider a particular case of the model of this section where $H(q^1, \ldots, q^N) = \Sigma_{i=1}^{N} q^i$ and where all the agents are identical. The efficient allocation for which all the agents have the same level of utility is then obtained by maximizing

$$U \left\{ x(Nq, C), q, R - \frac{C}{N} - c(q) \right\}. \tag{2.20}$$

Condition (2.15) takes the form

$$\frac{\partial U}{\partial x} \frac{\partial x}{\partial C} + \frac{\partial U}{\partial y} \left(-\frac{1}{N} \right) = 0$$

and conditions (2.16) and (2.17) take the form

$$\frac{\partial U}{\partial x} \frac{\partial x}{\partial (Nq)} N + \frac{\partial U}{\partial q} - \frac{\partial U}{\partial y} \frac{dc}{dq} = 0.$$

---

[13] In the case of pollution control, the term 'effluent charge' is prefered to 'toll'.

Up to now, we have considered N as a parameter, fixed *a priori*, on which we had no control. Thus, we could modify Q only by varying q. Now, let us consider N as a variable, the value of which is a matter of choice. In other words, consider that a much larger set of identical agents can be divided into subsets, each with the same size membership N, and that this size is a variable under our control, which we must choose optimally. Optimally, in this case, means in a way that will maximize (2.20) with respect not only to C and q, but also to N. By setting the derivative of (2.20) with respect to N to zero, we obtain the first-order condition:

$$\frac{\partial U}{\partial x}\frac{\partial x}{\partial (Nq)}q + \frac{\partial U}{\partial y}\frac{C}{N^2} = 0.$$

Due to (2.15), this may also be written

$$\frac{\partial x}{\partial (Nq)} + \frac{\partial x}{\partial C}\frac{C}{Nq} = 0$$

or, by (2.19),

$$\frac{C^{\cdot}}{Nq} = \frac{dC}{d(Nq)}. \tag{2.21}$$

This is the best known simple result provided by the theory of clubs: when all of the agents are identical, it is optimal to divide them into subsets, called 'clubs', so as to minimize in each club the average cost of the public good made available to the members of the club. The extension of this result to heterogeneous populations of agents is far from obvious; it forms the heart of the theory of clubs, which is outside the scope of this book.[14]

3. Non-traceable Sources and Indirect Instruments

All of the preceding discussion rests on the assumption that the public authority has the ability to act directly on the sources of pollution, through effluent charges, tolls, taxes, and/or standards. To do this it must be able to identify the contribution of each polluter towards the degradation of the environment. This is not always possible. Consider, for example, the pollution caused by fertilizers or by pesticides carried by water run-off or infiltration. Can indirect

[14] A detailed presentation is given in Cornes and Sandler (1986).

instruments, such as taxes on or subsidies for goods involved in the production or consumption processes that create the pollution, be useful? The response is guarded: such instruments are useful, but in general they are less efficient than instruments applied directly to emissions. In addition, they must often be applied in a way that is surprising on first view, for example as a subsidy to a good generating pollution.

To focus this general response, let us for instance consider N farms: all produce the same good (a cereal, for example) from two factors of production l and m (fertilizer and energy or labour). These N farms are too small for their supplies and demands to have a significant influence on the formation of prices, p, p_l, and p_m on the markets, respectively, for the good produced and for the factors of production l and m. In all of this section, these prices will therefore be considered as fixed. We also take the social cost τ of a unit of pollution as given.

There are two types of farms (according to the location and soil composition of their fields, for example), which differ both in their costs of production and in the pollution they create. For a quantity produced y, all farms of the type i ($i = 1, 2$) use the quantities of factors l and m

$$y_l^i = h^i(y)$$

and

$$y_m^i = \delta^i h^i(y),$$

where h^i are convex functions representing decreasing returns, and y_l^i and y_m^i are proportional, meaning that the factors l and m are strict complements; farm i's cost of production is therefore

$$C^i(y) = (p_l + \delta^i p_m) h^i(y). \tag{2.22}$$

Furthermore, each farm of type 1 creates a pollution ηy_l^1 proportional to the quantity y_l^1 of factor l which it uses (no technology of purification being available), while farms of type 2 do not create any pollution.[15]

If nothing is done to control the pollution, each farm, of whichever type, chooses the level of production y_ε^i that equalizes its marginal revenue and marginal costs:

$$p = C^{i'}(y_\varepsilon^i) = (p_l + \delta^i p_m) h^{i'}(y_\varepsilon^i). \tag{2.23}$$

[15] This hypothesis is made to simplify the presentation; the results require only that the two types be different in the ways they pollute.

This level is socially efficient for $i = 2$: y_e^2 is equal to y_c^2, the socially optimal level of production for type 2 farms. It is excessive for $i = 1$, because it does not consider the social cost of the pollution created; there is a non-controlled externality here. Of course, it would suffice to make each type 1 farm pay an effluent charge τ per unit of pollution, in other words $\eta\tau$ per unit of factor l that it uses. In this way, each type 1 farm would find it in its best interest to choose the socially efficient level of production y_c^1 which equalizes marginal revenue and marginal social cost:

$$p = C^{1'}(y_c^1) + \eta\tau h^{1'}(y_c^1) = (p_l + \delta^1 p_m + \eta\tau)h^{1'}(y_c^1). \qquad (2.24)$$

But sometimes it is not possible to identify who pollutes and by how much. For technical, legal or political reasons it may not be possible to detect individual polluters through the routes of their pollution. In these circumstances, the public authority has to devise measures which, although imposed in the same way upon the two categories of farms, induce reactions whose differences contribute as far as possible to reduce the externality. Thus the public authority, using its powers to tax or subsidize certain goods, can arrange that all farms are faced with prices P and P_l, rather than prices p and p_l, the differences $P - p$ and $P_l - p_l$ being the taxes or subsidies. If P and P_l are chosen so that

$$\frac{P}{P_l + \delta^1 p_m} = \frac{p}{p_l + \delta^1 p_m + \eta\tau} \qquad (2.25)$$

and so that

$$\frac{P}{P_l + \delta^2 p_m} = \frac{p}{p_l + \delta^2 p_m}, \qquad (2.26)$$

then each type of farm will react in the desired way, choosing y_c^i as its level of production $(i = 1, 2)$. What conditions (2.26) and (2.25) amount to can be reformulated in the following way: the ratio between price of product and cost of producing one unit is kept invariant for type 2 farms, whereas it is multiplied by less than 1 for type 1 farms, namely:

$$\frac{P}{P_l + \delta^1 p_m} = \lambda \frac{p}{p_l + \delta^1 p_m}$$

with

$$\lambda = \frac{p_l + \delta^1 p_m}{p_l + \delta^1 p_m + \eta\tau}.$$

While this is always possible algebraically, it is not always meaningful economically, because, as prices, P and p_l cannot be negative. Now, from (2.25) and (2.26), we see that

$$P = \frac{(\delta^1 - \delta^2)p_m}{(\delta^1 - \delta^2)p_m + \eta\tau} p \tag{2.27}$$

and

$$P_l = \frac{P}{p}p_l - \frac{\delta^2 p_m \eta\tau}{(\delta^1 - \delta^2)p_m + \eta\tau}. \tag{2.28}$$

To understand the economic meaning of these two formulae, let us consider two cases, $\delta^1 > \delta^2$ and $\delta^1 < \delta^2$.

First case: $\delta^1 > \delta^2$

Then P is positive. P_l is positive if and only if the ratio δ^1 to δ^2 is large enough, namely,

$$\frac{\delta^1}{\delta^2} > \frac{p_l + \eta\tau}{p_l}.$$

If this condition is met, there exist prices P and P_l generating the desired incentives; they are such that

$$P < p \qquad \text{and} \qquad P_l < p_l.$$

The factor of production that generates the pollution is therefore subsidized! This result, paradoxical at first glance, can be explained by the fact that replacing p_l by $P_l < p_l$ leads to a greater relative decrease of $p_l + \delta^2 p_m$ than of $p_l + \delta^1 p_m$, and hence is a greater advantage for the farms of type 2 than for those of type 1. All experience the same tax $p - P$ on their production.

Second case: $\delta^1 < \delta^2$

Then P is positive if and only if $(\delta^2 - \delta^1)p_m > \eta\tau$, in which case P_l is also positive, and we have

$$P > p \qquad \text{and} \qquad P_l > p_l.$$

The factor of production that generates the pollution is taxed, because that leads to a relative increase of $p_l + \delta^2 p_m$ which is smaller than that of $p_l + \delta^1 p_m$. Type 1 farms are thus more sensitive to the tax than type 2 farms, while both types benefit from the same subsidy $P - p$ per unit of good produced.

If P and P_l in (2.27) and (2.28) are not both positive, it is no longer possible to lead the farms by indirect methods to the optimal behaviour ('first-best' Pareto optimum) that could be induced by direct methods of intervention (as in Section 1). The public authority can still use indirect methods, but with a lesser ambition: to minimize the deviation from optimal behaviour, that is to achieve a second-best Pareto optimum.

Let us characterize such a second-best optimum with N types of economic agents (the farms). To lighten the notation, let us consider that there is one agent by type. At prices P and P_l, agent i decides to produce $y^i(P, P_l)$ determined by

$$P = (P_l + \delta^i p_m) h^{i\prime}(y_i). \tag{2.29}$$

Let $\varepsilon^i(P, P_l)$ be the difference between the social marginal value of i's production and the social marginal cost when the quantity $y_i(P, P_l)$ is produced, that is, the difference between p and $(p_l + \delta^i p_m + \eta^i \tau) h^{i\prime} \{y^i(P, P_l)\}$. Due to (2.29), this difference reads

$$\varepsilon^i(P, P_l) = p - \frac{(p_l + \delta^i p_m + \eta^i \tau) P}{P_l + \delta^i p_m}. \tag{2.30}$$

Then $\varepsilon^i \, dy^i$ measures the benefit of modifying by dy^i the production $y^i(P, P_l)$ of agent i. The only means available to induce this modification is indirect: it is to modify P or P_l, and hence to act simultaneously on the production decisions of the N agents.

If P is modified and becomes $P + dP$, that induces the modification

$$dy^i = \frac{\partial y^i(P, P_l)}{\partial P} dP,$$

to which corresponds the benefit

$$\varepsilon^i \, dy^i = \varepsilon^i(P, P_l) \frac{\partial y^i(P, P_l)}{\partial P} dP.$$

For the whole of the N agents, the total benefit is thus

$$\sum_{j=1}^{N} \varepsilon^j(P, P_l) \frac{\partial y^j(P, P_l)}{\partial P} dP.$$

This sum appears to be the average of the individual ε^i weighted by the production modifications induced by the change in P. Hence, there is no benefit to modifying P if

$$\sum_{j=1}^{N} \frac{\partial y^j(P, P_l)}{\partial P} \varepsilon^j(P, P_l) = 0. \tag{2.31}$$

Similarly, there is no benefit to modifying P_l if

$$\sum_{j=1}^{N} \frac{\partial y^j(P, P_l)}{\partial P_l} \varepsilon^j(P, P_l) = 0. \tag{2.32}$$

Conditions (2.31) and (2.32) are the first-order necessary conditions for the maximization, with respect to P and P_l, of the social value of the total production, i.e. of

$$\sum_{j=1}^{N} p y^j(P, P_l) - (p_l + \delta^j p_m + \eta^j \tau) h^j \{ y^j(P, P_l) \}. \tag{2.33}$$

They are necessary conditions for second-best optimality; with P and P_l as the only available instruments, it is usually not possible to induce behaviour leading to first-best optimality. Indeed, it is not possible in general to verify the conditions

$$\varepsilon^i(P, P_l) = 0, \quad i = 1, \ldots, N, \tag{2.34}$$

which generalize (2.25) and (2.26), and are necessary for first-best optimality. Only in special cases is it is possible to achieve a first-best optimum, using P and P_l. For example, if $N = 2$, the resolution in P and P_l of (2.34) gives

$$P = p \frac{(\delta^1 - \delta^2) p_m}{(\delta^1 - \delta^2) p_m + (\eta^1 - \eta^2) \tau}$$

$$P_l = \frac{(\delta^1 - \delta^2) \} p_l p_m + (\delta^1 \eta^2 - \delta^2 \eta^1) \tau p_m}{(\delta^1 - \delta^2) p_m + (\eta^1 - \eta^2) \tau}.$$

If these values, which generalize (2.27) and (2.28), are positive, then P and P_l can be used to induce each agent to produce at the optimal level (first-best optimality). However, we have stressed the limits of this result. In general, only some form of second-best optimality is within reach. As can be seen from a comparison between (2.31) and (2.32) on the one hand, and (2.34) on the other, necessary conditions respectively for second-best and first-best optimality have some resemblance, but still differ significantly. Second-best optimality is the central theme of the following two chapters; we shall have many opportunities to derive and discuss conditions for second-best optimality, showing in particular how and why they depart from the corresponding conditions for first-best optimality.

3
If You Can't Get a First, Aim at a Second-best Optimum

1. Making Up for the Inability to Price at Marginal Cost

A rail line that linked a suburban town to the centre of a large city lies disused. Reopening the line would allow the town residents to escape the trouble of road congestion when they get to the centre. There is no question that the expected benefits, net of operating costs, are high enough to warrant the fixed cost of putting the infrastructure of the line back into working conditions. This however does not ensure that it will be possible to cover the fixed cost, along with the operating costs, through the receipts of operating the line.[1] If it is equally impossible—for institutional or psychological reasons, or perhaps simply because there are too many people involved—to implement a decision process of the kind considered in Chapter 1, must the idea of reopening the line be abandoned? Or is it justified to search for other sources of support, even for sources that are not bound to the rail business?

Let us imagine, for example, that one could place services—booksellers, news agents, fast food—within the town station. A municipal decision would reserve the rights to this commerce for the authority in charge of running the line. The same decision would allow the authority to offer these services at prices high enough to contribute to the fixed cost of the line. Could such a decision be justified by arguments of economic efficiency, even though it seems to go against sound pricing practices? And does it not raise problems of distributive justice? To avoid ambiguity on these issues, we will

[1] In Figure 3.1, the users' benefits net of operating costs are measured by the area $c_j \bar{p}_j A_j^c$, while the receipts at price p_j net of operating costs are measured by the area $c_j p_j A_j B_j$. When the former are greater than the fixed cost, while for any p_j the latter are smaller, it is both desirable to reopen the line and impossible to raise enough money by simply charging the customers as they travel.

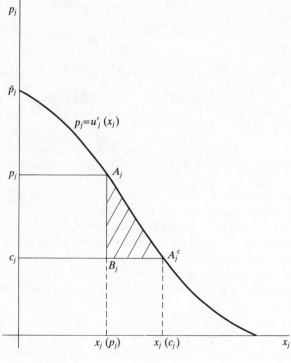

$$p_j = u'_j(x_j)$$

FIG. 3.1

concentrate on the first one in this chapter, postponing the second one to Chapter 4.

These questions are relevant even if it is actually possible to cover the fixed cost through the receipts of operating the line. Indeed, from the moment there is no means of reaching a first-best optimum,[2] the way to a second-best optimum is usually not to depend solely on one direct source of funding. A second-best optimum would result from a well-chosen mix of sources, contrary to recommendations that have been made by such diverse bodies as the EEC Commission, the Law Lords and HM Treasury in Britain, a Committee on transport policy appointed by the Prime Minister in France, etc.

Since in this chapter we intend to deal with the first question only ('Could such a decision be justified by arguments of economic

---

[2] I.e. a Pareto optimum in the usual sense (see ch. 1).

efficiency?'), it is possible and convenient to consider the case where the preferences of all the potential users of the rail line are the same and can be represented by the same utility function U. U depends on three variables: x_1, the number of kilometres travelled during a fixed period of time; x_2, the consumption of services offered in the town station, aggregated in a single category called 'service' or 'good' 2;[3] and y, all other consumption (as in Section 2 of Chapter 1). We will always normalize the prices so that y is the numeraire; i.e., the price of y is 1 throughout. In this section, we will simplify further by assuming that U is additively separable: there exist increasing, concave, and differentiable functions u_1 and u_2 such that

$$U(x_1, x_2, y) = u_1(x_1) + u_2(x_2) + y. \tag{3.1}$$

We can, without additional restriction, normalize U so that

$$u_1(0) = u_2(0) = 0. \tag{3.2}$$

For the consumer,[4] $u_j(x_j)$ is the amount of numeraire equivalent to x_j; substituting $u_j(x_j)$ units of numeraire for x_j units of good j leaves his utility level unchanged.

On the production side, the total cost of producing x_1 and x_2 is

$$C + c_1 x_1 + c_2 x_2 \tag{3.3}$$

where $c_j x_j$ is the variable cost of production of $x_j (j = 1, 2)$, while C is the fixed cost of production for the two goods. C can be decomposed into

$$C = C_1 + C_2 + C_{12} \tag{3.4}$$

where C_j is the fixed cost which can be imputed to good j, while C_{12} is a joint fixed cost. This means that the production of even the smallest quantity of good j, j being either 1 or 2, requires that $C_j + C_{12}$ be spent beforehand; the joint production of both goods thus requires that $C_1 + C_2 + C_{12}$ be spent beforehand.

Let p_j be the price set by the authority for good $j (j = 1, 2)$. The consumer's demand function for good j is then

$$x_j = x_j(p_j), \tag{3.5}$$

which is the inverse function of

$$p_j = u'_j(x_j). \tag{3.6}$$

---

[3] For all goods or services, we will use the word 'good'.
[4] We will use the words 'consumer' and 'user' equally. Speaking of 'the' consumer is possible, as all consumers here are identical.

The surplus $s_j(p_j)$, obtained by the consumer when buying the quantity $x_j(p_j)$ of good j at price p_j, is by definition the maximum amount of numeraire he would forgo beyond the amount $p_j x_j(p_j)$ that he pays the seller, in order to get hold of $x_j(p_j)$. Due to (3.1) and (3.2), the surplus is here[5] the utility of consuming $x_j(p_j)$ net of the corresponding payment:

$$s_j(p_j) = u_j\{x_j(p_j)\} - p_j x_j(p_j); \tag{3.7}$$

this is the area $p_j \bar{p}_j A_j$ under the demand curve $x_j(p_j)$ in Figure 3.1.

If it were possible, as in Section 2 of Chapter 1, to have the fixed cost paid from lump-sum contributions,[6] we could set prices $p_j = c_j$. They would lead each consumer to choose consumptions x_j^{opt} such that

$$c_j = u_j'(x_j^{\text{opt}}). \tag{3.6'}$$

This is a simplistic[7] application of the principle of pricing at marginal cost. To quickly check that the resulting consumption decisions x_j^{opt} are indeed optimal, consider the implications of a price p_j different from c_j. For p_j less than c_j, one must provide the producer with a subsidy $(c_j - p_j)x_j(p_j)$ per consumer. This subsidy is greater than the increase in surplus associated with the difference $c_j - p_j$. The net loss $L_j(p_j)$ that results is the area $A_j A_j^c B_j$ in Figure 3.2. On the other hand, a price p_j that is greater than c_j would produce a profit $(p_j - c_j)x_j(p_j)$, but this profit would be less than the decrease in surplus associated with the difference $p_j - c_j$. The resulting net loss is again the area $A_j A_j^c B_j$, this time in Figure 3.1. Hence, if it is possible to have the fixed cost paid from lump-sum contributions, then the prices $p_j = c_j$ are indeed optimal, in the first-best sense; if not, one must accept the losses that result from having the prices different from marginal costs, while seeking to minimize these losses.

Let us first consider prices $\hat{p}_j(j = 1, 2)$, which ensure budget balance good by good, i.e. which are such that

$$C_j = N(\hat{p}_j - c_j)\hat{x}_j$$

---

[5] Defining the consumer's surplus when the utility function is not additively separable is more complicated; see Section A2 of the Appendix.

[6] The contributions being lump-sum, no contributor can change the amount he has to pay by changing his behaviour in any way. The collection of lump-sum contributions has no distortive effects on resource allocation, contrary to income or consumption taxes.

[7] Simplistic because, with the cost function (3.3), the marginal cost is a constant c_j which is independent of the quantity x_j produced. On the optimality of pricing at marginal cost, see Section A1 of the Appendix.

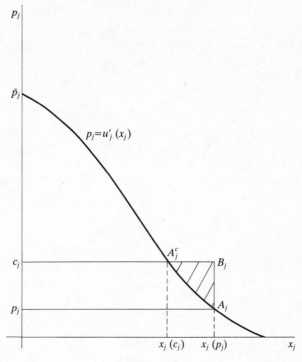

Fig. 3.2

where $\hat{x}_j = x_j(\hat{p}_j)$, and where N is the total number of consumers; for ease of exposition we take $C_{12} = 0$ here. Although such prices do not always exist, we assume here that they do. Then they allow each good to cover exactly its own costs, fixed and variable, through its receipts.

Now consider prices $p_j^* (j = 1, 2)$ such that

$$p_1^* < \hat{p}_1 \quad \text{and} \quad p_2^* > \hat{p}_2$$

and

$$C_1 - N(p_1^* - c_1)x_1^* = N(p_2^* - c_2)x_2^* - C_2 \tag{3.8}$$

where $x_j^* = x_j(p_j^*)$. These prices cover the production costs of both goods on a global basis. In the case represented in Figure 3.3, the prices p_j^* are preferable to the prices $\hat{p}_j$ because they induce demands x_j^* entailing less loss of total surplus $s_1 + s_2$ than the demands $\hat{x}_j$. Indeed, the increase in surplus for the consumer who acquires the

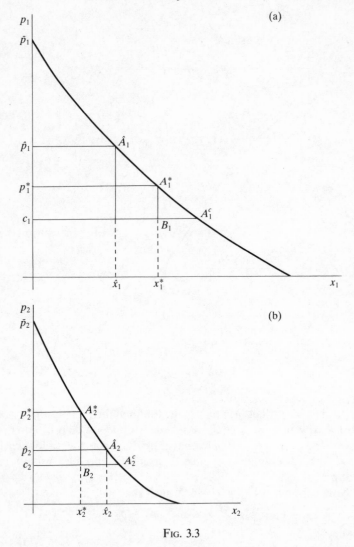

Fig. 3.3

quantity x_1^* of good 1 at price p_1^* rather than the quantity $\hat{x}_1$ at price $\hat{p}_1$ (this increase is the area $p_1^* \hat{p}_1, \hat{A}_1 A_1^*$ in Figure 3.3) is greater than the decrease in surplus resulting from the fact that he acquires the quantity x_2^* of good 2 at price p_2^* in place of $\hat{x}_2$ at price $\hat{p}_2$ (this decrease is the area $\hat{p}_2 p_2^* A_2^* \hat{A}_2$). If $\hat{p}_1$ does not exist, good 1 could not be offered without being supported by good 2; in this case, the comparison is between the areas $p_1^* \bar{p}_1 A_1^*$ and $\hat{p}_2 p_2^* A_2^* \hat{A}_2$.

It is therefore not desirable in general to aim at budget balance good by good, that is to stick to systems of prices similar to $\hat{p}_j$. Instead, one must consider all the price systems assuring global budget balance, and choose from among them a system of so-called second-best prices, i.e. prices associated with a second-best optimum. These prices prompt decisions that minimize the loss arising from the interaction of

— technical constraints: the cost functions are given and they include fixed costs;
— institutional constraints: it is not possible to raise lump-sum contributions;
— patterns of behaviour: consumption decisions are made at the individual level and depend on prices.

If it were possible to raise lump-sum contributions, or if there were no fixed cost, then pricing at marginal cost would be feasible and there would be no loss at all.

2. A Pricing Rule Compatible with Limited Freedom of Action

What conditions must be satisfied by second-best prices? We will answer this question on the basis of a quasi-linear utility function,

$$U(x_1, x_2, y) = u(x_1, x_2) + y, \qquad (3.9)$$

which allows for substitution effects between goods 1 and 2; u is an increasing, quasi-concave, and differentiable function in x_1 and x_2. But in keeping enough additive separability in (3.9), we still neglect income effects.[8] In this chapter we will stick to utility functions that are additively separable in the way (3.9) is.

Endowed with an amount R of numeraire—his initial income— and faced with prices p_1 and p_2 for goods 1 and 2, the consumer pursues his individual objective: to maximize U while satisfying the budget constraint

$$p_1 x_1 + p_2 x_2 + y = R, \qquad (3.10)$$

---

[8] Income effects are taken into account in sec. 3 of ch. 4. They are neglected here in the sense that the demands for goods 1 and 2 derived from a utility function like (3.9) do not depend on the income that the consumer has available, but only on the prices p_1 and p_2 at which those goods are sold.

to which he is subjected. His demand functions

$$x_j = x_j(p_1, p_2) \tag{3.11}$$

for goods $j = 1, 2$ satisfy the first-order necessary conditions for the constrained maximization of U; these read:

$$p_j = u'_j(x_1, x_2) \tag{3.12}$$

where

$$u'_j = \frac{\partial u}{\partial x_j}.$$

The amount y of numeraire left available for consumption is also a function of p_1 and p_2, namely (with high enough R)

$$y = R - p_1 x_1 - p_2 x_2 \tag{3.13}$$

where x_1 and x_2 are the demand functions for goods 1 and 2, as given in (3.11).

Consumers have no clear idea of how prices are set. Each of them realizes that he is a negligible quantity among the total population of N consumers. He is thus convinced that he cannot influence the choice of the prices, and he does not attempt any kind of strategic behaviour. He is a price-taker; he accepts the prices as given parameters in his economic environment, and he reacts to them as described by (3.12). These prices, on the other hand, are instruments for the authority in charge of producing goods 1 and 2, whose line of conduct is to make use of them in the best interest of the consumers, given the constraints that limit its freedom of action. From a precise formulation of this objective and these constraints, we will now derive how the authority should use the instruments, i.e. how it should set prices.

Consider any price system $p_j (j = 1, 2)$. The revenue, net of variable costs, that this price system raises is $NT(p_1, p_2)$, $T(p_1, p_2)$ being the revenue raised per consumer. T is the function of p_1 and p_2 given by

$$T = (p_1 - c_1)x_1 + (p_2 - c_2)x_2 \tag{3.14}$$

where x_1 and x_2 still are the demand functions[9] for goods 1 and 2. As no restriction has yet been put on the prices that we consider for the moment, there is no reason why NT should exactly match C.[10] In order to fill the gap between NT and C, a lump-sum contribution

---

[9] x_j is the individual demand; the total demand for good j is Nx_j.

[10] $C = C_1 + C_2 + C_{12}$ as in (3.4); here C_{12} (as well as C_1 or C_2) can take any non-negative value.

equal to $(C/N) - T$ should be raised from each consumer.[11] Suppose for a moment that this is possible. Then the consumer's initial income, i.e. his income available for spending on goods 1, 2 and the numeraire, would be $R - \{(C/N) - T\}$. Hence his utility level would be

$$V\left\{p_1, p_2, R - \left(\frac{C}{N} - T\right)\right\} = u\{x_1(p_1, p_2), x_2(p_1, p_2)\}$$

$$+ R - \left(\frac{C}{N} - T\right) - p_1 x_1(p_1, p_2)$$

$$- p_2 x_2(p_1, p_2); \tag{3.15}$$

at prices p_1 and p_2, and with the initial income $R - \{(C/N) - T\}$, the amount of numeraire left available for consumption is indeed

$$R - \left(\frac{C}{N} - T\right) - p_1 x_1(p_1, p_2) - p_2 x_2(p_1, p_2).$$

V is an indirect utility function; it is that function of prices and initial income which is derived from the direct utility function U by substituting for the consumer's decision variables x_1, x_2, and y the values resulting from the maximization of U subject to the budget constraint, i.e. the consumer's demands at the prices and initial income considered. V generalizes the surplus $s_1 + s_2$ defined in Section 1 of this chapter, where complete additive separability of the direct utility function was assumed.

If the prices p_j are set equal to marginal costs, V takes the value

$$V\left(c_1, c_2, R - \frac{C}{N}\right), \tag{3.16}$$

which is the first-best utility level,[12] i.e. the highest level compatible with the technical and resource constraints (the initial resources amount to NR). For any other price system, (3.15) is less than (3.16), and the difference

$$L(p_1, p_2) = V\left(c_1, c_2, R - \frac{C}{N}\right) - V\left\{p_1, p_2, R - \left(\frac{C}{N} - T\right)\right\} \tag{3.17}$$

[11] It may well be the case that NT is greater than C; then the required contribution is negative; i.e., a lump-sum payment is made to each consumer.

[12] Speaking of 'the' first-best utility level makes sense here, because all consumers are identical; it is the utility level associated with those Pareto-efficient allocations that treat all consumers equally.

is the loss[13] per consumer entailed by charging prices different from marginal costs. The derivative of L with respect to p_j is easily derived from (3.15), (3.14) and (3.12):

$$\frac{\partial L}{\partial p_j} = \frac{\partial}{\partial p_j}\left\{-u(x_1, x_2) + c_1 x_1 + c_2 x_2\right\}$$

$$= -(p_1 - c_1)\frac{\partial x_1}{\partial p_j} - (p_2 - c_2)\frac{\partial x_2}{\partial p_j}. \tag{3.18}$$

From the definition (3.14) of T, one immediately obtains

$$\frac{\partial T}{\partial p_j} = x_j + (p_1 - c_1)\frac{\partial x_1}{\partial p_j} + (p_2 - c_2)\frac{\partial x_2}{\partial p_j}$$

$$= x_j - \frac{\partial L}{\partial p_j}. \tag{3.19}$$

The quotient of these two derivatives, i.e. $(\partial L/\partial p_j)/(\partial T/\partial p_j)$, is the marginal loss incurred when raising an extra unit of numeraire through an increase in the price p_j.

As it is actually not possible to raise lump-sum contributions, the authority is limited to those price systems (p_1, p_2) that make NT match C:

$$NT(p_1, p_2) - C = 0. \tag{3.20}$$

This global budget constraint, similar to (3.8), precludes it from aiming at the first-best utility level $V\{c_1, c_2, R - (C/N)\}$; instead, its objective is to minimize the loss $L(p_1, p_2)$ subject to the constraint (3.20). This means solving in p_1 and p_2 the optimization problem

$$\min_{p_1, p_2} L(p_1, p_2)$$

$$\text{s.t. } \frac{C}{N} - T(p_1, p_2) = 0. \tag{3.21}$$

Using γ to indicate the multiplier associated with the global budget constraint, the Lagrangean for this problem reads:

$$\mathcal{L}(p_1, p_2; \gamma) = L(p_1, p_2) + \gamma\left\{\frac{C}{N} - T(p_1, p_2)\right\}.$$

By setting the derivatives of the Lagrangean with respect to the

---

[13] In the case represented in Figure 3.3, owing to the complete additive separability of the utility function, the loss $L(p_1, p_2)$ is the sum of two components $L_1(p_1)$ and $L_2(p_2)$. For $p_1 = p_1^*$ and $p_2 = p_2^*$, for instance, $L_1(p_1^*)$ is represented by the area $A_1^* A_1^c B_1$, and $L_2(p_2^*)$ by the area $A_2^* A_2^c B_2$.

variables $p_j (j = 1, 2)$ to zero, we obtain the first-order necessary conditions for the constrained optimization problem (3.21):

$$\frac{\partial \mathscr{L}}{\partial p_j} = \frac{\partial L}{\partial p_j} - \gamma \frac{\partial T}{\partial p_j} = 0. \tag{3.22}$$

From (3.19), these conditions read

$$(1 + \gamma) \frac{\partial L}{\partial p_j} - \gamma x_j = 0.$$

Hence from (3.18) we get

$$\frac{(p_1 - c_1) \dfrac{\partial x_1}{\partial p_j} + (p_2 - c_2) \dfrac{\partial x_2}{\partial p_j}}{x_j} = -\frac{\gamma}{1 + \gamma}.$$

Because of the separability in (3.9), i.e. because there is no income effect, we have

$$\frac{\partial x_1}{\partial p_2} = \frac{\partial x_2}{\partial p_1}.$$

Hence the first-order necessary conditions can be rewritten:

$$\frac{(p_1 - c_1) \dfrac{\partial x_j}{\partial p_1} + (p_2 - c_2) \dfrac{\partial x_j}{\partial p_2}}{x_j} = -\frac{\gamma}{1 + \gamma}. \tag{3.23}$$

As it is equivalent to minimize $L(p_1, p_2)$ subject to constraint (3.20), or to maximize $V(p_1, p_2, R)$ subject to the same constraint, conditions (3.22) or (3.23) might have been derived from

$$\begin{aligned} &\max_{p_1, \, p_2} V(p_1, p_2, R) \\ &\text{s.t. } T(p_1, p_2) - \frac{C}{N} = 0. \end{aligned} \tag{3.24}$$

By setting to zero the derivatives of the Lagrangean for this maximization, with δ as the multiplier associated with the constraint, we obtain the first-order necessary conditions:

$$\frac{\partial V}{\partial p_j} + \delta \frac{\partial T}{\partial p_j} = 0. \tag{3.22'}$$

But from (3.15), (3.12), and (3.19), we have

$$\frac{\partial V}{\partial p_j} = -\frac{\partial}{\partial p_j} (L + T).$$

Conditions (3.22') can thus be rewritten:

$$\frac{\partial L}{\partial p_j} - (\delta - 1) \frac{\partial T}{\partial p_j} = 0.$$

These are the conditions (3.22) with

$$\delta = 1 + \gamma. \tag{3.25}$$

Conditions (3.22), or the equivalent conditions (3.22'), or also (3.23), are called the Ramsey–Boiteux conditions.[14] They are conditions on the prices that the authority sets: to secure a second-best optimum, the authority must set prices that satisfy the Ramsey–Boiteux conditions; such prices are second-best prices. Written under the form (3.22), the Ramsey–Boiteux conditions mean that, at a second-best optimum, the marginal loss incurred when raising an extra unit of numeraire through a price increase is independent from the price being increased; the multiplier γ measures this marginal loss. From (3.25), δ thus appears as the shadow price of the resources (in numeraire) made available to the authority: when one unit of numeraire is transferred from the consumer to the authority, the cost to the consumer is that unit plus the loss γ. Hence, written under the form (3.22'), the Ramsey–Boiteux conditions express the equality between price (i.e. δ) and marginal opportunity cost (i.e. $-(\partial V/\partial p_j)/(\partial T/\partial p_j)$).

Written under the form (3.23), the Ramsey–Boiteux conditions can be given an interpretation in terms of price elasticities of demand. Let

$$\varepsilon_{jk} = \frac{\partial x_j/\partial p_k}{x_j/p_k}, \qquad j = 1, 2; \ k = 1, 2 \tag{3.26}$$

be the elasticity of demand for good j with respect to price k, i.e. the percentage increase in demand for good j by percentage increase in the price of good k. For $j = k$, ε_{jj} is normally negative; for $j \neq k$, ε_{jk} is positive or negative depending on goods j and k being substitutes or complements. Conditions (3.23) then read:

$$\tau_1 \varepsilon_{j1} + \tau_2 \varepsilon_{j2} = -\frac{\gamma}{1 + \gamma} \tag{3.23'}$$

where

$$\tau_k = \frac{p_k - c_k}{p_k} \tag{3.27}$$

[14] After. Ramsey (1927) and Boiteux (1956). For recent surveys, see Guesnerie (1980) and Bös (1985).

is the toll, or tax, rate[15] on good k. When the utility function is of the form (3.1), i.e. is additively separable also between x_1 and x_2, then $\varepsilon_{12} = \varepsilon_{21} = 0$ and conditions (3.23′) have a particularly simple interpretation: at a second-best optimum, toll rates and price elasticities are inversely proportional. For more general utility functions, those of the form (3.9), conditions (3.23′) also express a relationship between toll rates and price elasticities; although more complicated, this relationship is of practical use, as we will see in Section 3.

The conclusion that has been drawn in Section 1, for the case represented in Figure 3.3, from the comparison between prices p_j^* and $\hat{p}_j$ is of general validity, provided p_j^* are second-best prices. Then the difference between the areas $p_1^*\hat{p}_1\hat{A}_1A_1^*$ (or $p_1^*\bar{p}_1A_1^*$ if $\hat{p}_1$ does not exist) and $\hat{p}_2p_2^*A_2^*\hat{A}_2$ represents indeed the additional loss—in regard to the second-best optimum corresponding to the prices p_j^*—which would be caused by the obligation to finance separately the costs of production of the two goods.

3. Some Traps into which Common Sense May Fall

In a Memorandum on transport policy addressed in March 1971 to the member-states, the EEC Commission made strong recommendations on pricing rules:

Each mode of transportation, and, within each of these modes, each category of users, must cover through its own means the totality of costs which are imputable to it. This precludes all aid from public funds as well as all subsidy of one activity by another.

A few years later, the French Prime Minister was given a consonant piece of advice by a committee[16] that he had appointed to

---

[15] In the situation considered at the beginning of this chapter, the rights to open shops within the railway station have been reserved to the authority in charge of the line. It would have come to the same thing to grant these rights to private entrepreneurs, to tax the goods they sell in such a way that the prices paid by the consumers satisfy the Ramsey–Boiteux conditions, and to transfer the revenue from these taxes to the railway authority. A more general model with tolls, taxes, and subsidies is considered in ch. 4.

[16] Known as the Commission Guillaumat, after the name of the chairman, who was head of one of the ten largest French firms and who had been a defence minister under Général de Gaulle. The report, from which the above lines are taken, was published in 1978 by La Documentation Française, the French counterpart of HMSO in Britain or the US Government Printing Office; it has been circulated to a large audience.

provide him with broad orientations for transport policy:

If pricing at marginal cost represented an important progress, methodologically and practically, it nevertheless appears insufficient as a foundation for efficient and stable conditions of competition between different modes of transportation. These must rest, in the opinion of the Committee, on a pricing method which makes the users of each category of infrastructure support the totality of the costs which it entails.

By definition, the fixed costs of a mode of transportation are fixed in the sense that they cannot be modified except by the complete suppression of this mode. As soon as a mode is operated, the intensity of its use is without influence on the fixed costs, and hence no incentive to a better utilization can be obtained by making 'the users of each category of infrastructure support the totality of the costs it entails'.

In reality, the best utilization (first-best optimum) would be obtained by confronting the users with marginal costs. When this is impossible, a second-best optimum does not result from the exact covering by each mode of all of its costs through its receipts; it results from charging second-best prices, i.e. prices for which the Ramsey–Boiteux conditions are satisfied.

Let us take the form (3.23′) of these conditions and eliminate γ; we then have

$$\tau_1(-\varepsilon_{11}+\varepsilon_{21})=\tau_2(\varepsilon_{12}-\varepsilon_{22}). \tag{3.28}$$

Let good 1 be transport by rail in a country, and good 2 be transport by road, and suppose there is only one global budget constraint common to rail and road; i.e., suppose there is a public authority endowed with the power of transferring financial resources from rail to road or vice versa. What kind of transfer is then advisable? Empirical studies show that ε_{21} is negligible and that $-\varepsilon_{11}$ is greater than, or approximately equal to, $\varepsilon_{12}-\varepsilon_{22}$. On the other hand, condition (3.28) implies that, if $-\varepsilon_{11}+\varepsilon_{21}$ is greater than or equal to $\varepsilon_{12}-\varepsilon_{22}$, the same is true for the rate τ_2 in relation to τ_1. The desirability of transferring financial resources from road to rail then results from two facts: the rates are applied to rather different demands, much greater for road than for rail, whereas fixed costs are greater for rail than for road. In France, at the time the Commission Guillaumat was reporting to the Prime Minister, the optimal total amounts per mode that should havé been raised were actually in the proportion of one-sixth for rail and five-sixth for road. Since the fixed costs were in the proportion of two-thirds for rail and one-third for road, second-best optimality required that three-fourths of the fixed costs of rail be paid for through resources raised from road traffic.

We will complete this section by using the Ramsey–Boiteux conditions to assess the impact on the consumers of an improvement in the techniques of production; we will see how this impact depends on the prevailing institutional arrangements. In the model of Section 2 above, we now introduce a second producer, who produces only good 2 and whom we call B. We call A the producer who was already present in the model (i.e. the authority in charge of the rail line); A jointly produces goods 1 and 2 and must balance his budget. The two techniques also differ in that:

— B has no fixed cost, but has the same variable cost as A;
— B has a limited capacity of production S, and this capacity is less than the size of the market for good 2; i.e., S is less than the total demand for good 2 at all relevant prices.

Producer B aims at profit-maximizing and is not subject to any tax. With respect to A, B behaves as a follower, taking as given the price p_2 of good 2, and on this basis maximizing his profit. The result is that B sells S—the maximum quantity he can produce—at price p_2[17] and makes a profit $(p_2 - c_2)S$. This profit is shared between the consumers.

At given prices p_1 and p_2, A's receipts net of variable costs (per consumer) are thus reduced from $T(p_1, p_2)$ to:

$$T_s(p_1, p_2) = (p_1 - c_1)x_1 + (p_2 - c_2)\left(x_2 - \frac{S}{N}\right)$$

$$= T(p_1, p_2) - (p_2 - c_2)\frac{S}{N}. \tag{3.29}$$

On the other hand, the loss L remains unchanged, because the decrease in T and the transfer of B's profit to the consumers offset

[17] More accurately, at a price $p_2 - \varepsilon$, which is slightly less than p_2.

each other:

$$L_s(p_1, p_2) = V\left(c_1, c_2, R - \frac{C}{N}\right) - V\left\{p_1, p_2, R + (p_2 - c_2)\frac{S}{N}\right.$$

$$\left. - \left(\frac{C}{N} - T_s\right)\right\} = L(p_1, p_2). \tag{3.30}$$

The Ramsey–Boiteux conditions, which A must satisfy when setting second-best prices, thus read:

$$\frac{\partial L_s}{\partial p_j} - \gamma_s \frac{\partial T_s}{\partial p_j} = 0. \tag{3.31}$$

Using (3.29) and (3.30), it is possible to rewrite them in terms of L and T:

$$\frac{\partial L}{\partial p_1} - \gamma_s \frac{\partial T}{\partial p_1} = 0$$

and

$$\frac{\partial L}{\partial p_2} - \gamma_s \left(\frac{\partial T}{\partial p_2} - \frac{S}{N}\right) = 0.$$

How does a second-best optimum, supported by second-best prices $\tilde{p}_1$ and $\tilde{p}_2$ satisfying conditions (3.31) compare with one supported by second-best prices satisfying conditions (3.22)? As B's profit is shared between the consumers, and as A makes no profit, the comparison is between utility levels.

The presence of B on the market reduces the set of feasible prices, worsening the result of the optimization. Another way to see it is to imagine that, for some reason, B's capacity is decreased by a small amount dS. Then each consumer's income is decreased by $(\tilde{p}_2 - c_2)dS$, whereas T is increased by the same amount: it is as if a lump-sum contribution were raised from the consumer and given to A, hence reducing the necessary amount of tolls. As γ_s is the marginal loss per unit of numeraire raised through tolls, the gain in utility for the consumer is $\gamma_s(\tilde{p}_2 - c_2)dS$. Going on decreasing S, and modifying the second-best prices accordingly, further increases the utility level until the second-best optimum supported by the prices p_1^* and p_2^* is restored for $S = 0$.

This shows that B's entry in the market will hurt the consumers unless B's marginal cost is smaller than c_2 by a sufficiently large margin. It is not enough that B offers an improvement in the conditions of production of good 2; this improvement must be large enough to offset the more exacting effects of the institutional constraints. Other institutional arrangements, for example the possibility of taxing B's output, would change the situation.

Until now, we have implicitly ruled out the possibility that no prices exist that would satisfy conditions (3.31). However, it may be the case that prices that provide A with enough revenue to cover all its costs do exist when A supplies the totality of the demand for good 2, but do not exist when A is deprived from a share of size S: then A can no longer function, good 1 disappears, and the loss for the consumers can be large. This is the kind of loss that Kahn (1966) had in mind when, under the title 'The Tyranny of Small Decisions', he wrote:

The event that first suggested the phenomenon to this writer was the disappearance of passenger railroad service from Ithaca, a small and comparatively isolated (since that time even more so!) community in upstate New York. It may be assumed the service was withdrawn because over a long enough period of time the individual decisions travellers made, for each of their projected trips into and out Ithaca and the other cities served, did not provide the railroad [with] enough total revenue to cover costs. Considering the comparative comforts and speeds of competing media, those individual decisions were by no means irrational: the railroad was slow and uncomfortable. What reason, then, was there to question the aggregate effect of those individual choices—withdrawal of the service? The fact is that the railroad provided the one reliable means of getting into and out of Ithaca in all kinds of weather. Hence this inadequately used alternative was something I for one would have been willing to pay something to have kept alive.[18]

[18] At that time the author was professor of economics at Cornell University (Ithaca). Later he was appointed chairman of the Civil Aeronautic Board by President Carter. In his example the competing firms offer not the same good, but substitutes, and there is no capacity constraint; but the effect is similar. Here firm A is the railroad and the two goods it offers are passenger rail service in winter and passenger rail service in other seasons, the latter being in competition with air travel.

4

Fair Taxes and Fares

1. Efficient Taxes and Fares

London, 17 December 1981. Front page of *The Standard*:

CHEAP FARES OUTLAWED
Law Lords rule: Fares Fair illegal, London Transport 'must balance its books'.

London, 30 June 1982. Leader of *The Times*:

LONDON TRANSPORT'S FALLING DOWN
The Law Lords' interpretation of the Transport (London) Act 1969 was by definition conclusive in law, but it was not an instructed framework for a transport policy. An urgent national debate is needed leading to major national legislation over the legitimate level and nature of subsidy and the way it should be shared between local and national taxation.

In an election held in May 1979, the Labour Party had won the majority in the Greater London Council (GLC). Enforcing one of the main points in their election manifesto, they introduced the so-called 'Fares Fair' scheme for running London Transport: more frequent buses and Underground trains, fares reduced by about 30 per cent, zonal system greatly simplified. As a result, the total number of travellers increased significantly, although not enough to meet the whole of the extra costs. To finance the necessary subsidy, the GLC increased local taxes in the Greater London area. The London Borough of Bromley, a Tory stronghold, applied to the High Court for judicial review of these GLC initiatives. Having failed in the High Court, Bromley went to the Court of Appeal, where it won. The case was settled on 17 December 1981, by the Law Lords.

The consequences were immediate—a 60 per cent increase in fares—and devastating for London Transport. To quote *The Times* once again, 'The service is far advanced in operational decay.' In this chapter we examine some contributions that economic analysis can make to a debate of the kind urged by *The Times*. To that end, we will broaden the model used in Chapter 3.

In this broadened model, there are J private goods and K public goods.[1] Among the private goods, those labelled $j = 1, \ldots, J_c$ are produced by competitive firms; their production entails no fixed cost. They are thus sold by the producing firms at their respective marginal costs; however, consumers will in general buy them at higher prices, as taxes will be added. The other private goods, those labelled $j = J_c + 1, \ldots, J$, are produced jointly: their production entails a fixed cost C as well as variable costs. As in Chapter 3, for all J private goods we will take the variable costs as proportional to the respective quantities produced (i.e., the marginal costs are constant), and we will denote these constant marginal costs by $c_j (j = 1, \ldots, J)$.

As for the K public goods, they are produced at a total cost $C(\mathbf{z})$, the component z_k of the vector $\mathbf{z}$ being the quantity that is produced of public good $k (k = 1, \ldots, K)$. $C(\mathbf{z})$ is increasing in each z_k; we place no other restriction on C than differentiability. The public goods are made available to the consumers by a public authority (PA), which also sets taxes on the competitively produced private goods, and which controls the joint production of the other private goods.

There are N identical consumers with utility function

$$U(\mathbf{x}, y, \mathbf{z}) = u(\mathbf{x}, \mathbf{z}) + y \qquad (4.1)$$

where $\mathbf{x}$ is the vector whose J components are the quantities of the private goods consumed by the representative consumer. U has the usual properties; in this section, moreover, we keep assuming additive separability between u and the quantity y of numeraire consumed; i.e., we neglect income effects, which will be dealt with in Section 3. Endowed with an initial income R, and faced with the price vector $\mathbf{p}$, whose J components are the prices of the private goods, the consumer maximizes U subject to the budget constraint

$$\mathbf{p}\mathbf{x} + y = R.$$

His demand functions

$$\mathbf{x} = \mathbf{x}(\mathbf{p}, \mathbf{z}) \qquad (4.2)$$

satisfy the first-order necessary conditions for the constrained maximization of U, i.e.

$$p_j = u_j'(\mathbf{x}, \mathbf{z}),$$

[1] We introduced the distinction between private and public goods in ch. 1.

where

$$u'_j = \frac{\partial u}{\partial x_j}, \qquad j = 1, \ldots, J.$$

These demand functions depend not only on the prices of the private goods, but also on the available quantities of the public goods. The public goods indeed interact with the private goods in the consumer's utility function.[2] The amount y of numeraire left available also depends on $\mathbf{p}$ and $\mathbf{z}$:

$$y(\mathbf{p}, \mathbf{z}) = R - \mathbf{p}\mathbf{x}(\mathbf{p}, \mathbf{z}). \tag{4.3}$$

The consumer's indirect utility function is thus

$$V(\mathbf{p}, R; \mathbf{z}) = u\{\mathbf{x}(\mathbf{p}, \mathbf{z}), \mathbf{z}\} + R - \mathbf{p}\mathbf{x}(\mathbf{p}, \mathbf{z}). \tag{4.4}$$

The joint production of the private goods $j = J_c + 1, \ldots, J$, is subject to the budget constraint

$$N \sum_{i=J_c+1}^{J} (p_i - c_i) x_i(\mathbf{p}, \mathbf{z}) + S = C \tag{4.5}$$

where S is a subsidy from (or to, when S is negative) the overall budget of the PA. This overall budget is itself subject to the constraint

$$N \sum_{i=1}^{J_c} t_i x_i(\mathbf{p}, \mathbf{z}) = S + C(\mathbf{z}) \tag{4.6}$$

where t_j is the tax imposed on good $j(j = 1, \ldots, J_c)$. For all private goods it will be convenient to use the notation

$$p_j = c_j + t_j,$$

p_j being the price paid by the consumers and t_j the tax or the toll, depending on whether $j = 1, \ldots, J_c$ or $j = J_c + 1, \ldots, J$.

The best policy that the PA can pursue under these circumstances is to maximize the indirect utility (4.4) subject to constraints (4.5) and (4.6); this is indeed equivalent to minimizing the loss arising from the distortions that result from the imposition of taxes and tolls.[3] The instruments available to the PA are the taxes and tolls (or, equivalently, the prices $\mathbf{p}$), the quantities $\mathbf{z}$ of the public goods, and the

---

[2] For instance, the level of public safety in a city influences the utility derived from attending theatre performances or films, from patronizing shops or restaurants, etc. The demands for these services thus depend on the prevailing level of public safety.

[3] Here we assume that there are no other distortions in the economy than those which result from the imposition of taxes and tolls, and that the latter affect only consumption decisions, not production decisions; later in this section we will reconsider these assumptions.

subsidy S. R is not an instrument, but a fixed parameter, because we rule out the possibility for the public authority to levy lump-sum contributions. This might seem odd, in the case of an economy where all consumers are identical; but this case is merely a preliminary one, and when dealing with it we must have in mind the generalization to the case of an economy with different types of consumers. The optimization problem for the PA thus reads:

$$\max_{\mathbf{p}, \mathbf{z}, S} V(\mathbf{p}, R; \mathbf{z}) \tag{4.7}$$

s.t.

$$\sum_{i=J_c+1}^{J} (p_i-c_i)\, x_i(\mathbf{p}, \mathbf{z})+\frac{S}{N}-\frac{C}{N}=0$$

and

s.t.

$$\sum_{i=1}^{J_c} (p_i-c_i)\, x_i(\mathbf{p}, \mathbf{z})-\frac{S}{N}-\frac{C(\mathbf{z})}{N}=0.$$

Using δ to designate the multiplier associated with the first constraint and δ_c the multiplier associated with the second one, and setting to zero the derivative of the Lagrangean with respect to S, we get

$$\delta-\delta_c=0. \tag{4.8}$$

This condition means that, at a second-best optimum, the shadow price of the financial (i.e. expressed in numeraire) resources made available to the PA is the same whether these resources are obtained through taxes or through tolls.

Setting to zero the derivatives of the Lagrangean with respect to p_j ($j=1, \ldots, J$) and to z_k ($k=1, \ldots, K$), we have the first-order necessary conditions for the constrained optimization problem (4.7):

$$\frac{\partial V}{\partial p_j}+\delta\frac{\partial T}{\partial p_j}=0. \tag{4.9}$$

and

$$\frac{\partial V}{\partial z_k}+\delta\frac{\partial T}{\partial z_k}-\frac{\delta}{N}\frac{\partial C}{\partial z_k}=0. \tag{4.10}$$

where

$$T=\sum_{i=1}^{J} (p_i-c_i)\, x_i(\mathbf{p}, \mathbf{z}).$$

Owing to the additive separability between u and y in the utility function, conditions (4.9) can be rewritten as

$$\sum_{i=1}^{J} t_i \frac{\partial x_j}{\partial p_i} = \frac{1-\delta}{\delta} x_j. \tag{4.9'}$$

These, or equivalently (4.9), are the Ramsey–Boiteux conditions. As for conditions (4.10), they can be rewritten as

$$N\frac{\partial V}{\partial z_k} = \delta \left\{ \frac{\partial C}{\partial z_k} - \sum_{i=1}^{J} t_i \frac{\partial(Nx_i)}{\partial z_k} \right\}. \tag{4.10'}$$

These conditions generalize the Samuelson conditions for efficiency in the production of public goods introduced in Section 2 of Chapter 1. The left-hand side of (4.10') is indeed the total willingness to pay for a marginal increase in z_k. Within the brackets of the right-hand side, we have the difference between the marginal cost of producing public good k and, on the other hand, the marginal net revenue from the increases in the total demands of the J private goods, prompted by a marginal increase in z_k. This difference is thus the net strain on the PA financial resources from a marginal increase in z_k. As δ is the shadow price of such resources, (4.10') is a marginal benefit–cost rule for second-best efficiency in the production of public goods.

In this spirit, all ministerial departments, local governments, public firms, etc., in France have been reminded by the Treasury that: 'the shadow price of public funds bears on all expenditures supported—directly or indirectly—by the public budget. This is due to the global nature of the financial constraint which limits public investments and to its lasting character.' If it happens that the cost of producing a public good is small compared with the total amount of public expenditures, then it might be expedient to consider—as is often the case in practice—that δ does not depend upon the decision about this particular good. Rather, δ is determined by the general policy on public finance, and can be communicated to whoever has the production of the public good in charge, for him to decide according to (4.10').

Each of the Ramsey–Boiteux conditions (4.9) is also a marginal benefit–cost rule, balancing losses or gains to the consumers and net revenue to the PA, both resulting from the same marginal change in the level of a tax or a toll. All these necessary conditions for second-best optimization thus take a form well-known in microeconomics, that of an equality between marginal benefit and marginal cost of an action. In order to get yet another useful interpretation of the Ramsey–Boiteux conditions, consider a marginal uniform intensification of all taxes and tolls; i.e., consider modifications dt_j of the taxes and tolls that are proportional to the values t_j to which they apply:

$$\frac{dt_j}{t_j} = \varepsilon, \qquad j = 1, \ldots, J;$$

ε is a convenient notation for the common value of all dt_j/t_j considered. These modifications induce the following changes in the demands for private goods:

$$dx_j = \sum_{i=1}^{J} \frac{\partial x_j}{\partial p_i} t_i \varepsilon.$$

Conditions (4.9′) may then be rewritten:

$$\frac{dx_j}{x_j} = \frac{1-\delta}{\delta} \varepsilon. \tag{4.9″}$$

Under the form (4.9″), the Ramsey–Boiteux conditions mean that, at a second-best optimum, the percentage reductions in demands that result from a marginal uniform intensification of all taxes and tolls are the same for all J private goods.[4] This is very different from claiming that tax and toll rates must be uniform, as did the British Government in 1971 when it asked Parliament to vote the introduction of a value added tax in the United Kingdom: 'By discriminating less between different goods and services, a more broadly-based structure would reduce the distortion of consumer choice. Selective taxation gives rise to distortion of trade and of personal consumption patterns, and can lead to an inefficient allocation of resources.'[5]

Up to now, we have assumed that the distortions resulting from the imposition of taxes and tolls affect only the consumption decisions. To what extent are the necessary conditions for second-best optimality modified when production decisions are also affected? To answer this question, let us specialize the previous model to the case where there are only two private goods, goods 1 and 2, besides the numeraire. They are produced by competitive firms, and they entail no fixed cost. There is one public good. Let us then introduce one

---

[4] The numeraire is of course left apart, as it is never subject to any tax nor toll.
[5] HMSO, 1971, Cmnd. 4621; quoted from Atkinson and Stiglitz (1980, 366).

modification regarding production processes: in order to produce good 1, firm 1 now needs two inputs, the numeraire and good 2.

Firm 1 indeed produces good 1 according to the following production function:

$$x_1 = g(y^1, x_2^1) \tag{4.11}$$

where g is differentiable, quasi-concave, and homogeneous of degree one. The latter property means that good 1 is produced with constant returns to scale: multiplying by the same factor k both the quantity y^1 of numeraire and the quantity x_2^1 of good 2 put into the production of good 1 has the effect of also multiplying by k the output x_1. This is a direct generalization of the previous production function $x_1 = (1/c_1)y^1$, which meant that good 1 was produced from the numeraire at constant marginal cost c_1. As far as good 2 is concerned, we keep that simple form: good 2 is still produced (by firm 2) from the numeraire only, at constant marginal cost c_2.

How does firm 1 choose the mix of inputs it uses to produce one unit of good 1? Faced with a price p_2 for good 2 and, of course, a price equal to 1 for the numeraire, firm 1 minimizes its cost of production by choosing quantities y^1 and x_2^1 of inputs so as to satisfy (4.11) and

$$\frac{\partial g/\partial x_2^1}{\partial g/\partial y^1} = p_2. \tag{4.12}$$

Let us designate the resulting y^1 and x_2^1 by

$$y^1 = y^1(p_2) \quad \text{and} \quad x_2^1 = x_2^1(p_2);$$

they do indeed depend on the price p_2 at which firm 1 buys good 2. In order to produce x_1 units of good 1, firm 1 thus uses quantities of numeraire and of good 2 that are, respectively,

$$x_1 y^1(p_2) \quad \text{and} \quad x_1 x_2^1(p_2);$$

these are firm 1's demands for inputs.

Now both firms behave competitively and have constant returns to scale; hence they make no profit. On the other hand, the goods they produce, respectively goods 1 and 2, are subject to taxes t_1 and t_2. The consumer[6] then buys good 2 at the price

$$p_2(t_2) = c_2 + t_2 \tag{4.13}$$

---

[6] Because consumers are identical and there are constant returns to scale in the production of both goods, it does not matter whether we take one or N consumers: the mix of inputs chosen by firm 1 does not change, and it is in this mix that we are interested here.

and good 1 at the price

$$p_1(t_1, t_2) = y^1\{p_2(t_2)\} + p_2(t_2)x_2^1\{p_2(t_2)\} + t_1$$
$$= c_1(t_2) + \theta_1(t_1, t_2). \tag{4.14}$$

In (4.14) we use the following notations:

$$c_1(t_2) = y^1\{p_2(t_2)\} + c_2 x_2^1\{p_2(t_2)\} \tag{4.15}$$

is the value of resources (expressed in numeraire) used by firm 1 to produce one unit of good 1 when it buys good 2 at price p_2; and

$$\theta_1(t_1, t_2) = t_1 + t_2 x_2^1\{p_2(t_2)\} \tag{4.16}$$

is the amount of taxes paid by the consumer when he buys one unit of good 1. From (4.11) and (4.12), we have

$$\frac{\mathrm{d}y^1}{\mathrm{d}p_2} + p_2\frac{\mathrm{d}x_2^1}{\mathrm{d}p_2} = 0;$$

hence[7]

$$\frac{\partial p_1}{\partial t_2} = x_2^1. \tag{4.17}$$

The loss that results from the imposition of the taxes t_1 and t_2 is

$$L(t_1, t_2) = V\left\{c_1(0), c_2, z, R - \frac{C(z)}{N}\right\}$$
$$- V\left[p_1(t_1, t_2), p_2(t_2), z, R - \left\{\frac{C(z)}{N} - T(t_1, t_2)\right\}\right].$$

with

$$T(t_1, t_2) = \theta_1(t_1, t_2)\left[x_1\{p_1(t_1, t_2), p_2(t_2), z\}\right]$$
$$+ t_2[x_2\{p_1(t_1, t_2), p_2(t_2), z\}].$$

The derivatives of L with respect to t_1 and t_2 are

$$\frac{\partial L}{\partial t_1} = -\theta_1\frac{\partial x_1}{\partial p_1} - t_2\frac{\partial x_2}{\partial p_1}$$

$$\frac{\partial L}{\partial t_2} = \left(-\theta_2\frac{\partial x_1}{\partial p_2} - t_2\frac{\partial x_2}{\partial p_2}\right) + x_2^1\frac{\partial L}{\partial t_1} + x_1\frac{\mathrm{d}c_1}{\mathrm{d}t_2}.$$

The term within the brackets in $\partial L/\partial t_2$ is the usual one: it corresponds to the distortion induced on the consumption decisions x_1 and x_2 by the tax t_2 through its effect on the price p_2. The term $x_2^1(\partial L/\partial t_1)$ corresponds to the distortion induced on the same decis-

---

[7] We will no longer explicitly indicate the dependence in t_1 or in t_2.

ions by the tax t_2 through its effect on the price p_1. The last term corresponds to the distortion induced by the tax t_2 on the decision that firm 1 takes regarding the mix of inputs it uses.

The first-order necessary conditions for minimizing the loss L, subject to the global budget constraint $NT - C(z)$, are the usual ones:

$$\frac{\partial L}{\partial t_j} - \gamma \frac{\partial T}{\partial t_j} = 0, \qquad j = 1, 2. \tag{4.18}$$

However, deriving from (4.18) a form analogous to (4.9′) makes the effect of t_2 on production decisions appear explicitly:

$$\theta_1 \frac{\partial x_1}{\partial p_1} + t_2 \frac{\partial x_2}{\partial p_1} = -\frac{\gamma}{1+\gamma} x_1$$

$$\theta_1 \frac{\partial x_1}{\partial p_2} + t_2 \frac{\partial x_2}{\partial p_2} - x_1 \frac{dc_1}{dt_2} = -\frac{\gamma}{1+\gamma} x_2. \tag{4.18′}$$

When firm 1 buys good 2 at a price p_2 different from the marginal cost c_2, it inevitably chooses an inefficient mix of inputs to produce good 1. This inefficiency might be eliminated only by setting $p_2 = c_2$, i.e. $t_2 = 0$. But, as conditions (4.18′) show, $p_2 = c_2$ is not a second-best price: to accept a certain amount of production inefficiency entails a smaller loss than to put the whole burden of financing $C(z)$ on t_1. Things are different if it is possible to dissociate the taxation of good 2, when used as an input in the production of good 1, from the taxation of the same good when used as a final consumption good; this requires some monitoring of the transactions on good 2, in order to prevent tax evasion. Such a dissociation is a fundamental characteristic of the value added tax. Then a second-best optimum is obtained by not taxing good 2 at all when used as an input in the production of good 1[8]—hence ensuring production efficiency— while confronting the consumers with prices p_1 and p_2 that satisfy the conditions (4.18′) with $\theta_1 = t_1$ and $c_1 = c_1(0)$. This means that p_1 and p_2 then satisfy the Ramsey–Boiteux conditions (4.9′).

We have always assumed that there are no other distortions in the economy than those resulting from the imposition of taxes and tolls. We will not try to investigate in any systematic way the consequences of changing this assumption; that is beyond the scope of this

---

[8] A straightforward way to make up for the lost revenue would be to increase t_1 so that p_1 would remain unchanged. But the resulting situation is not yet a second-best optimum: it can still be improved upon.

book. We will limit ourselves to an example that illustrates the greater diversity of functions assigned to second-best prices in an economy where distortions are present prior to the imposition of any tax or toll. In this example we have one firm, say the firm producing good 1, that has a non-competitive behaviour: it sells good 1 at a price q_1 greater than the corresponding marginal cost c_1 (there is no fixed cost in the production of good 1).

Consider another good, say good 2, whose producer behaves competitively, selling at marginal cost c_2. If the two goods are substitutes, a tax should then be imposed on good 2 even when the PA need not raise financial resources through taxes and tolls, i.e. when the PA budget constraint is not binding. Imposing a tax on good 2 indeed increases the demand for good 1, hence mitigating the restrictive effect on that demand arising from the mark-up $q_1 - c_1$; thus, pricing good 2 at marginal cost would not be in the interest of consumers who must buy good 1 above marginal cost. The tax on good 2 should not however be too great; otherwise the effect on the demand for good 2 would be more detrimental than the effect on the demand for good 1 is beneficial.

In the more general case, where the PA budget constraint is binding and where also distortions are present in the economy prior to the imposition of taxes or tolls, these would have two types of functions at a second-best optimum:[9] providing the PA with the required financial resources, and partly correcting the pre-existing distortions.

2. Form and Weight of Distributive Objectives

As long as we stick to an economy where all consumers are identical, the only relevant issue is to maximize the results of economic activity, which all consumers enjoy equally. When different types of consumers coexist, we cannot even define precisely what should be maximized without considering how the results are shared. To appraise the significance of this link, the simple case of an economy with two types of consumers will do. In this economy, there are N^m (identical) consumers of type $m (m = 1, 2)$, and each of them has a

---

[9] Hagen (1979) provides a clear and careful analysis of those two types of functions and of how they interact.

direct utility function similar[10] to (4.1):

$$U^m(\mathbf{x}^m, y^m) = u^m(\mathbf{x}^m) + y^m \tag{4.19}$$

and therefore an indirect utility function of the form (4.4):

$$V^m(\mathbf{p}, R^m) = u^m\{\mathbf{x}^m(\mathbf{p})\} + R^m - \mathbf{p}\mathbf{x}^m(\mathbf{p}). \tag{4.20}$$

As for the overall budget constraint of the PA, it can be written

$$\sum_{m=1}^{2} N^m T^m(\mathbf{p}) = C \tag{4.21}$$

with

$$T^m(\mathbf{p}) = \sum_{i=1}^{J} (p_i - c_i) x_i^m(\mathbf{p}).$$

We make use of (4.8) to deal simultaneously with taxes and tolls.

We can imagine that the PA policy consists in maximizing, with the prices as instruments, some welfare function, subject to the constraint (4.21). But what welfare function? The answer is not obvious, whereas it is with a single type of consumers; then the welfare function is the individual utility function. A graphic presentation (see Figure 4.1) is easy for $J = 2$, $N^1 = N^2 = 1$, and it clearly shows in what way the answer is not obvious. Figure 4.1 actually comprises two figures, which are related in the following way: to each point (p_1, p_2) in Figure 4.1(a), there corresponds a point (V^1, V^2) in Figure 4.1(b) through the indirect utility functions

$$V^1 = V^1(p_1, p_2, R^1) \quad \text{and} \quad V^2 = V^2(p_1, p_2, R^2).$$

Let $A(p_1, p_2)$ designate that point. Now consider the line $\bar{p}_1 \bar{p}_2$ from the point $(\bar{p}_1, c_2)$ to the point $(c_1, \bar{p}_2)$ in Figure 4.1(a); it represents the set of price vectors (p_1, p_2) satisfying the budget constraint (4.21). To that line corresponds line $\bar{A}^2 \bar{A}^1$ in Figure 4.1(b), from the point $\bar{A}^2 = A(\bar{p}_1, c_2)$ to the point $\bar{A}^1 = A(c_1, \bar{p}_2)$. For each $m = 1, 2$, let (p_1^{*m}, p_2^{*m}) be a vector of prices that maximize $V^m(p_1, p_2, R^m)$, subject to constraint (4.21), and let A^{*m} be the corresponding point on $\bar{A}^1 \bar{A}^2$:

$$A^{*m} = A(p_1^{*m}, p_2^{*m}).$$

Among all feasible points, A^{*m} is the most favourable to consumer

---

[10] We ignore the dependence in $\mathbf{z}$, which would not bring any significant new result here.

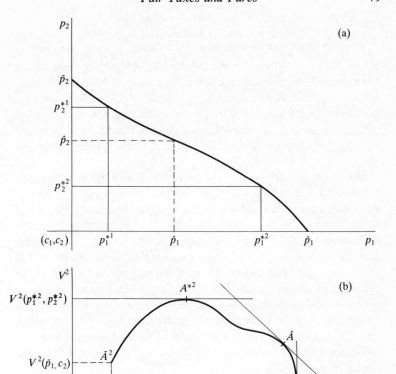

F$_{\text{IG}}$. 4.1

$m,$[11] with utility level

$$V^m(p_1^{*m}, p_2^{*m}, R^m) = \max_{p_1, p_2} V^m(p_1, p_2, R^m)$$

s.t. (4.21).

---

[11] Figure 4.1 is drawn with consumer 1 being more interested in good 1 and consumer 2 more interested in good 2. This is for example the case when $U^m = a_1^m \log x_1^m + a_2^m \log x_2^m$, with $a_1^1 + a_2^1 = a_1^2 + a_2^2$ and $a_1^1 > a_2^1$.

Except under exceptional circumstances, A^{*1} and A^{*2} are different.

No doubt it is efficient to choose p_1 and p_2 within, respectively, $[p_1^{*1}, p_1^{*2}]$ and $[p_2^{*1}, p_2^{*2}]$, i.e. $A(p_1, p_2)$ between A^{*1} and A^{*2} on $\bar{A}^1 \bar{A}^2$. But how to be more selective? Along $A^{*1}A^{*2}$, the interests of the two consumers are contradictory, consumer 1 favouring a smaller p_1 and consumer 2 a smaller p_2. It is not possible to select a particular point on $A^{*1}A^{*2}$ on the sole grounds of efficiency. $A^{*1}A^{*2}$ is the second-best utility possibility frontier, i.e. the utility possibility frontier of an economy subject to the budget constraint (4.21).

We might nevertheless be tempted to favour point $\hat{A}$, corresponding to point $(\hat{p}_1, \hat{p}_2)$ on $\bar{p}_1 \bar{p}_2$. It is indeed at $\hat{A}$ that the sum of utilities is maximized, subject to the budget constraint (4.21), or in other words it is at $\hat{A}$ -that the sum of losses arising from the distortions created by the imposition of taxes and tolls is minimized. But this way of presenting things is misleading, since to choose $\hat{A}$ is not only to implement a criterion of efficiency, but also to accept the distributive consequences that this criterion automatically brings about. At the individual level, the fact that the sum of the losses is minimized at $\hat{A}$ does not erase the preference that consumer m has for A^{*m}. At the collective level, it might be the case that one wants to enforce a criterion of distributive justice that does not lead to the choice of $\hat{A}$.

Before pushing ahead on the formulation of such a criterion, and so that we may be able to assess its impact in both efficiency and distributive terms, let us characterize more precisely the choice of $\hat{A}$, without being bound to the case of Figure 4.1. To determine $\hat{A}$—which is not necessarily unique—is to maximize

$$W(\mathbf{p}) = \sum_{m=1}^{2} N^m V^m(\mathbf{p}, R^m) \qquad (4.22)$$

subject to the budget constraint (4.21). The first-order necessary conditions for this constrained optimization problem read

$$\frac{\partial W}{\partial p_j} + \delta \frac{\partial T}{\partial p_j} = 0, \qquad j = 1, \ldots, J, \qquad (4.23)$$

with

$$T(\mathbf{p}) = \sum_{m=1}^{2} N^m T^m(\mathbf{p}).$$

These conditions still express, for each instrument p_j, and in terms of the specific objective pursued, the equality between marginal benefit and marginal cost of modifying the value of that instrument.

But the realization of this objective may well entail, in the final distribution of incomes,[12] socially unacceptable consequences. Expressing the collective will, the PA may for example aim at avoiding an excessive difference between incomes in the final distribution: the highest income, say $V^1(\mathbf{p}, R^1)$, should not exceed a certain multiple g of the lowest income, $V^2(\mathbf{p}, R^2)$. To ensure that maximizing W does not violate this criterion of distributive justice, a second constraint must be added to (4.21):

$$V^1(\mathbf{p}, R^1) \leqslant g V^2(\mathbf{p}, R^2), \tag{4.24}$$

with $g \geqslant 1$.

The optimization problem for the PA thus becomes:

$$\max_{\mathbf{p}} W(\mathbf{p}) \tag{4.25}$$

s.t. (4.21) and (4.24).

Using δ and λ to indicate the multipliers associated with constraints (4.21) and (4.24), the Lagrangean for this problem reads

$$\mathcal{L}(\mathbf{p}; \delta, \lambda) = W(\mathbf{p}) + \delta\{T(\mathbf{p}) - C\}$$
$$+ \lambda\{g V^2(\mathbf{p}, R^2) - V^1(\mathbf{p}, R^1)\}.$$

By setting to zero the derivatives of the Lagrangean with respect to the variables p_j ($j = 1, \ldots, J$), we obtain the first-order necessary conditions

$$\frac{\partial \mathcal{L}}{\partial p_j} = \frac{\partial W}{\partial p_j} + \delta\frac{\partial T}{\partial p_j} + \lambda\frac{\partial}{\partial p_j}(g V^2 - V^1) = 0. \tag{4.26}$$

As constraint (4.24) is an inequality, we have an additional necessary condition

$$\lambda(g V^2 - V^1) = 0;$$

hence λ is zero at an optimum where $g V^2$ is strictly greater than V^1. If this is the case at a solution $\hat{\mathbf{p}}$ of the problem (4.22), $\hat{\mathbf{p}}$ is obviously a solution of the problem (4.25): maximizing W subject to the sole budget constraint meets the criterion of distributive justice (4.24).

When $\lambda > 0$, things are not so simple. First, we must be able to

---

[12] The initial distribution of incomes is (R^1, R^2). We call $\{V^1(\mathbf{p}, R^1), V^2(\mathbf{p}, R^2)\}$ the final distribution of incomes resulting from $\mathbf{p}$; because of the additive separability of the utility functions, V^1 and V^2 are indeed measured in units of numeraire.

interpret the multiplier λ itself. In order to do so, imagine that the constraint (4.24) is replaced by

$$H(\mathbf{p}) + \varepsilon \geqslant 0 \qquad (4.27)$$

where

$$H(\mathbf{p}) = gV^2(\mathbf{p}, R^2) - V^1(\mathbf{p}, R^1).$$

According to whether ε is positive or negative, (4.27) is less or more constraining than (4.24). Let us designate by $\bar{W}(\varepsilon)$ the maximum value attained by W when maximized subject to the constraints (4.21) and (4.27); $\bar{W}$ is of course increasing in ε. By virtue of a theorem called, in optimization theory, the envelope theorem,[13] we have

$$\lambda = \frac{\mathrm{d}W}{\mathrm{d}\varepsilon},$$

the derivative being calculated at $\varepsilon = 0$. In general terms, we can say that the multiplier λ, more precisely the value it takes at an optimum for the problem (4.25), measures in terms of W the marginal benefit from being able at that optimum to relax constraint (4.27), with which λ is associated.

We now are in a position to interpret conditions (4.26), which may be rewritten

$$\frac{\partial W}{\partial p_j} + \delta\frac{\partial T}{\partial p_j} + \lambda\frac{\partial H}{\partial p_j} = 0. \qquad (4.26')$$

A change $\mathrm{d}p_j$ in p_j has a direct effect on W, i.e. $(\partial W/\partial p_j)\mathrm{d}p_j$, and an indirect one, i.e. $\lambda(\partial H/\partial p_j)\mathrm{d}p_j$. The change in p_j indeed relaxes the constraint $H \geqslant 0$ by $\mathrm{d}\varepsilon = (\partial H/\partial p_j)\mathrm{d}p_j$; we have just seen that the corresponding effect in terms of W is $\lambda\mathrm{d}\varepsilon$. Hence the marginal benefit, in terms of W, of changing p_j (think for example of a decrease in p_j) is

$$\frac{\partial W}{\partial p_j} + \lambda\frac{\partial H}{\partial p_j}.$$

On the other hand, the marginal cost, in terms of public revenue, is $-(\partial T/\partial p_j)$; δ being the shadow price of public revenue, the same cost in terms of W is

$$-\delta\frac{\partial T}{\partial p_j}.$$

Conditions (4.26) or (4.26') thus have the usual interpretation in terms of marginal benefits and costs of modifying a price.

[13] See Varian (1984, Appendix 13).

The Ramsey–Boiteux conditions (4.26) or (4.26′) are significantly different from their counterparts in Section 1, because they reflect concerns that are not relevant in an economy where all consumers are identical. But they are of the same nature: they mean that an objective is optimized only if the algebraic sum of all marginal benefits and costs, measured in terms of that objective, is zero for any modification of the prices—which are used as instruments in the optimization—associated with the claimed optimum.

The approach that has been taken to the interaction between efficiency and distributive considerations is easy to formulate, owing to the simple structure of both the objective to be optimized (W) and the criterion of distributive justice (g). But this approach has two flaws. First, it takes a rather particular view of distributive justice. Second, a solution p^* to the problem (4.25) may be inefficient, in the sense that it is sometimes possible to modify p^* to the simultaneous advantage of both types of consumers without violating the budget constraint (4.21). For example, in Figure 4.1, for any value of g larger than a threshold $\bar{g}$ corresponding to the straight line passing through the origin and A^{*2}, no point on the utility possibility frontier is compatible with constraint (4.24). For these reasons we will make use in the next section of more elaborate tools to deal with efficiency and distributive issues simultaneously.

3. General Ramsey–Boiteux Conditions on Taxes and Fares

Going back to the model of Section 1, we will successively relax two assumptions that we made at that stage: (1) there is no income effect on the consumption decisions; and (2) all consumers are identical. To do this, we will need a few concepts and results from the general theory of the consumer. These are gathered in Section A2 of the Appendix; readers might like to have a glance at that section before turning to the present one. We will first keep assumption (2) but relax assumption (1): there are here N identical consumers with an increasing, quasi-concave, and differentiable utility function of the general form $U(\mathbf{x}, y, \mathbf{z})$, y being the quantity of numeraire consumed.[14] As indirect utility function corresponding to U, let us choose the money-metric utility $\Psi(\mathbf{c}, 1; \mathbf{p}, 1, R; \mathbf{z})$, where $\mathbf{c}$ is the vector of

---

[14] By definition, the price of the numeraire is 1 throughout.

constant marginal costs c_j and **p** the vector of prices p_j for all J private goods other than the numeraire. In what follows, we will simply write $\Psi(\mathbf{c};\ \mathbf{p},\ R;\ \mathbf{z})$, without explicitly mentioning 1 as price of the numeraire.

The optimization problem for the PA is (4.7) with Ψ instead of V. Taking (4.8) into account, it is

$$\max_{\mathbf{p},\,\mathbf{z}} \Psi(\mathbf{c};\ \mathbf{p},\ R;\ \mathbf{z}) \tag{4.28}$$

$$\text{s.t. } T(\mathbf{p},\ \mathbf{z}) - \frac{C}{N} - \frac{C(\mathbf{z})}{N} = 0.$$

Conditions (4.9) and (4.10) do not change apart from Ψ replacing V. In terms of the equivalent[15] lump-sum contribution ϕ, conditions (4.9) read

$$\frac{\partial \phi}{\partial p_j} = \delta \frac{\partial T}{\partial p_j}. \tag{4.29}$$

When the price p_j is increased by dp_j, the corresponding fall in the consumer's utility level is measured by the increase $(\partial\phi/\partial p_j)dp_j$ in the equivalent lump-sum contribution ϕ. It is also the case that $(\partial\phi/\partial p_j)/(\partial T/\partial p_j)$ is the marginal increase in the equivalent lump-sum contribution that results from raising an extra unit of numeraire by increasing the price p_j. The Ramsey–Boiteux conditions (4.29) thus mean that, at a second-best optimum, the same marginal fall in utility level—measured in terms of the equivalent lump-sum contribution—is incurred when raising an extra unit of numeraire whatever the price being increased; the multiplier δ is this common value.

As Ψ is an indirect utility function to which Roy's identity applies, the Ramsey–Boiteux conditions can be rewritten under the form

$$-\frac{\partial \Psi}{\partial R} x_j + \delta \left(x_j + \sum_{i=1}^{J} t_i \frac{\partial x_i}{\partial p_j} \right) = 0$$

or

$$\sum_{i=1}^{J} t_i \frac{\partial x_i}{\partial p_j} = \left(-1 + \frac{1}{\delta} \frac{\partial \Psi}{\partial R} \right) x_j.$$

---

[15] As explained in Section A2 of the Appendix, the equivalence is in the following sense: the consumer enjoys the same level of utility when faced with prices c_j for the goods $j = 1, \ldots, J$, while having the initial income $R - \phi(\mathbf{p})$, as he does when faced with prices p_j while having the initial income R.

The Slutsky conditions and the symmetry of the Slutsky matrix then lead to

$$\sum_{i=1}^{J} t_i \frac{\partial x_j^c}{\partial p_i} = \left(-1 + \frac{1}{\delta}\frac{\partial \Psi}{\partial R} + \sum_{i=1}^{J} t_i \frac{\partial x_i}{\partial R} \right) x_j$$

or

$$\frac{\sum_{i=1}^{J} t_i \dfrac{\partial x_j^c}{\partial p_i}}{x_j^c} = -1 + \frac{1}{\delta}b \tag{4.29'}$$

with

$$b = \frac{\partial \Psi}{\partial R} + \delta \sum_{i=1}^{J} t_i \frac{\partial x_i}{\partial R}.$$

The quantity b of numeraire is the net marginal social benefit of (extra) income accruing to the consumer; it is net in the sense that the effect on the PA budget is taken into account.[16] As b is independent of j, the Ramsey–Boiteux conditions (4.29') mean that, at a second-best optimum, the percentage reduction in compensated demand that results from a marginal uniform intensification of all taxes and tolls is the same for all J private goods. Expressing this result in terms of compensated demands is appropriate: compensated demands reflect substitution effects, with income effects being neutralized, and these substitution effects actually are the forces behind the distortions in the consumption decisions, hence behind the compromises embodied in a second-best optimum.

Let us now assume that the N consumers have different initial incomes R^n and different preferences between goods consumed, hence different money-metric utilities Ψ^n. We also assume that the objective pursued by the PA is the maximization of some social welfare function $W(\Psi^1, \ldots, \Psi^N)$, which is quasi-concave, differentiable, and increasing in the individual utilities Ψ^n;[17] the social welfare function integrates both efficiency and distributive concerns.

---

[16] This will be discussed at greater length later in this section, when we consider non-identical consumers.

[17] It is a way of weighting the individual utilities, which generalizes the case of linear combinations of the form $\Sigma_{n=1}^{N} \lambda^n \Psi^n$, with $\Sigma_{n=1}^{N} \lambda^n = N$. From the definition of W, it results immediately that a solution to the optimization problem (4.30) is a second-best Pareto optimum, i.e. a Pareto optimum subject to the usual scarcity constraints plus the budget constraint $T(\mathbf{p}, \mathbf{z}) - C(\mathbf{z}) - C = 0$. Welfare functions are discussed in Atkinson and Stiglitz (1980).

The optimization problem for the PA thus reads:

$$\max_{\mathbf{p,z}} W(\mathbf{p,z}) \tag{4.30}$$

$$\text{s.t. } T(\mathbf{p,z}) - C(\mathbf{z}) - C = 0$$

with

$$T(\mathbf{p,z}) = \sum_{n=1}^{N} \sum_{i=1}^{J} t_i x_i^n(\mathbf{p,z}).$$

The first-order necessary conditions have the usual form and interpretation as marginal benefit–cost rules:

$$\frac{\partial W}{\partial p_j} + \delta \frac{\partial T}{\partial p_j} = 0 \tag{4.31}$$

$$\frac{\partial W}{\partial z_k} + \delta \frac{\partial T}{\partial z_k} - \delta \frac{\partial C}{\partial z_k} = 0. \tag{4.32}$$

Applying Roy's identity to each indirect utility function Ψ^n, we rewrite the Ramsey–Boiteux conditions (4.31) under the form

$$-\sum_{n=1}^{N} \frac{\partial W}{\partial \Psi^n} \frac{\partial \Psi^n}{\partial R^n} x_j^n + \delta \sum_{n=1}^{N} \left(x_j^n + \sum_{i=1}^{J} t_i \frac{\partial x_i^n}{\partial p_j} \right) = 0$$

or

$$\sum_{i=1}^{J} t_i \sum_{n=1}^{N} \frac{\partial x_i^n}{\partial p_j} = -\sum_{n=1}^{N} x_j^n + \frac{1}{\delta} \sum_{n=1}^{N} \frac{\partial W}{\partial \Psi^n} \frac{\partial \Psi^n}{\partial R^n} x_j^n.$$

The Slutsky conditions and the symmetry of the Slutsky matrix then lead to the form

$$\sum_{i=1}^{J} t_i \sum_{n=1}^{N} \frac{\partial x_j^{nc}}{\partial p_i} = -\sum_{n=1}^{N} x_j^n + \frac{1}{\delta} \sum_{n=1}^{N} \frac{\partial W}{\partial \Psi^n} \frac{\partial \Psi^n}{\partial R^n} x_j^n + \sum_{i=1}^{J} t_i \sum_{n=1}^{N} \frac{\partial x_i^n}{\partial R^n} x_j^n$$

or

$$\frac{\sum_{i=1}^{J} t_i \frac{\partial X_j^c}{\partial p_i}}{X_j^c} = -1 + \frac{1}{\delta} \varrho_j \tag{4.31'}$$

where

$$X_j^c = \sum_{n=1}^{N} x_j^{nc}$$

is the total compensated demand for good j,

$$\varrho_j = \sum_{n=1}^{N} b^n \frac{x_j^n}{\sum_{m=1}^{N} x_j^m}$$

is the distributional characteristic of good j, and

$$b^n = \frac{\partial W}{\partial \Psi^n} \frac{\partial \Psi^n}{\partial R^n} + \delta \sum_{i=1}^{J} t_i \frac{\partial x_i^n}{\partial R^n}$$

is the net marginal social benefit of income accruing to consumer n.

In order to grasp the economic meaning of b^n and ϱ_j, let us consider that the economy is at a second-best optimum; hence the Ramsey–Boiteux conditions (4.31′) are satisfied. Let us then suppose that an extra unit of numeraire comes as a windfall from outside the economy and that the PA is free to give it to any of the consumers, say n. This marginal increase in consumer n income has two effects, whose combination generates the net marginal social benefit b^n of income accruing to him:

— the social welfare function is increased by $(\partial W/\partial \Psi^n)(\partial \Psi^n/\partial R^n)$, which is the marginal social benefit of income accruing to consumer n;
— his purchases change, and in turn make his tax payments change, by the amount $\Sigma_{i=1}^{J} t_i(\partial x_i^n/\partial R^n)$, which accrues to the PA budget; the resulting marginal social benefit is here $\delta\Sigma_{i=1}^{J} t_i(\partial x_i^n/\partial R^n)$.

The distributional characteristic ϱ_j of good j is thus a weighted average over the N consumers of the respective b^n; the weights are their relative shares in the total consumption of good j. The larger the shares of consumers with a high net marginal social benefit of income, the greater ϱ_j is. Hence—and this is the interpretation of the Ramsey–Boiteux conditions (4.31′)—at a second-best optimum, the percentage reduction in total compensated demand for good j that results from a marginal uniform intensification of all taxes and tolls is lower, the larger the shares in the consumption of good j that go to the consumers with a high net marginal social benefit of income.

5
The Discipline of Potential Competition

1. Promise and Danger of Natural Monopoly

In 1981, William J. Baumol, then president of the American Economic Association, devoted his address at the annual meeting of the Association to what he called 'an uprising in the theory of industry structure'. Indeed, he asserted,

our analysis provides a generalization of the concept of the perfectly competitive market, one which we call a perfectly contestable market . . . The heroes are the potential entrants who exercize discipline on the incumbent, and who do so most effectively when entry is free. In the limit, when entry and exit are completely free, efficient incumbent monopolists and oligopolists may in fact be able to prevent entry. But they can do so only by behaving virtuously, that is, by offering consumers the benefits which competition would otherwise bring.[1]

These are great expectations: potential competition would make it possible to avoid the bureaucratic burden of regulation or nationalization, and yet to enjoy the benefits of increasing returns without having to suffer the drawbacks of unchecked monopolistic power. Baumol himself is cautious not to raise undue expectations. In a subsequent paper he stressed that contestability theory

[does not] offer carte blanche to mindless deregulation and dismantling of antitrust safeguards. On the contrary, so far as policy is concerned, contestability theory provides guidance in ascertaining where intervention is warranted socially, and it provides a more widely applicable benchmark to guide regulatory agencies and the courts in those arenas where intervention is called for by considerations of economic welfare.[2]

---

[1] This address was later published in the *American Economic Review* (Baumol 1982).
[2] Baumol and Willig (1986).

Potential competition has been described as a renewed form of invisible hand. In this chapter we will illustrate the sort of public policy that might help this invisible hand fulfil its potentialities. Ideally, we should consider a firm jointly producing a number of goods, as does the public firm considered in Chapter 4. But here this firm—call it firm A—is not public,[3] nor even regulated; A is a private firm seeking to maximize its profit while facing the prospect of competition from rival firms; each of these is in a position to produce, albeit less efficiently, some of the goods produced by A or substitutes for these goods. We should then examine the functioning of competition in this framework and, more specifically, ask ourselves whether rival firms may prevent A from behaving as an unconstrained monopoly, even if they are not active in the market. In other words, we should examine how potential competition may obtain and check A's monopoly power.

This programme is however far too ambitious; a whole book would no suffice to complete it. We will therefore answer the questions we have raised about the nature and effects of competition in a much more limited framework: firm A produces only one good, itself called good A, and faces but one competitor, firm B, which produces good B. Goods A and B are produced in discrete units, and consumers purchase at most one indivisible unit of one of the goods. Thus, a typical consumer[4] faces three choices: not to purchase anything, to purchase one unit of good A, or to purchase one unit of good B. Finally, we assume that A is a good of better quality than B; that is, if the price for both goods were identical, then all consumers would buy good A rather than good B. Examples of such goods might be: a flight between two cities at a given time, in more (A) or less (B) satisfactory conditions of speed and comfort; a personal computer, more (A) or less (B) powerful; etc. Corresponding examples of situations that might lead to potential competition are that of an airline, already active on a certain number of other connections, which considers opening a new line between the two aforementioned cities; or a firm, already selling minicomputers, which considers

---

[3] In ch. 4, we took for granted that the public firm always behaves according to public interest. In those circumstances where this assumption is too far from reality, it might indeed be more in the public interest to have a private monopoly constrained by potential competition, rather than an unanswerable public monopoly.

[4] It would be appropriate here to speak of a prospective consumer; however, for exposition purposes we shall not explicitly distinguish between actual and prospective consumers.

entering the market of personal computers. That firm, and the airline so described, play the role that firm B is to play throughout this chapter.

There is a continuum of consumers represented by the interval $[0, l]$. Consumer $x = 0$ has reservation values a for good A and b for good B, with $a > b > 0$. Consumer $x = l$ has the same reservation value b for good B, but his reservation value for good A is higher, namely $a + \eta$, with $\eta > 0$. As for consumers located between 0 and l, they all have b as their reservation value for good B, but their reservation value for good A is intermediate between a and $a + \eta$: consumer x, with $0 \leqslant x \leqslant l$, has the reservation value $a + (x/l)\eta$ for good A (see Figure 5.1 for an illustration). Thus, all consumers attach the same value to good B, whereas the preference for A varies in intensity, depending on where consumers are located on the line. This variation is intrinsic; it is not due to differences in income but to differences in the use different consumers can make of the superiority of good A over good B.

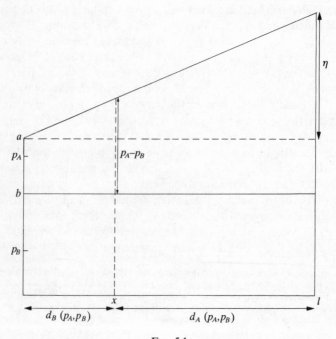

Fig. 5.1

Consumption choices will obviously depend on the prices p_A and p_B at which goods A and B are offered. Consumer x purchases nothing if $p_A > a + (x/l)\eta$ and $p_B > b$; otherwise, he purchases a unit of A if $a + (x/l)\eta - p_A$ is greater than $b - p_B$, and a unit of B in the opposite case. The (total) demand functions, for $p_A \leqslant a + \eta$ and $p_B \leqslant b$, will therefore be

$$d_A(p_A, p_B) = 0 \qquad \text{if } p_A \geqslant p_B + \eta + a - b$$

$$= \frac{l}{\eta}(\eta - p_A + a + p_B - b) \qquad \begin{aligned} &\text{if } p_B + \eta + a - b \geqslant p_A \\ &\qquad\qquad \geqslant p_B + a - b \end{aligned} \qquad (5.1)$$

$$= l \qquad \text{if } p_B + a - b \geqslant p_A$$

$$d_B(p_A, p_B) = l - d_A(p_A, p_B). \qquad (5.2)$$

In the case where $p_A \leqslant a + \eta$ but $p_B > b$, there is no demand for good B, firm A is alone serving the market, and the demand function for good A is

$$d_A^m(p_A) = d_A(p_A, b). \qquad (5.3)$$

In the case where $p_B \leqslant b$ but $p_A > a + \eta$, there is no demand for good A and all consumers purchase B; i.e.,

$$d_B^m(p_B) = l. \qquad (5.4)$$

It should be stressed that, in this model, where an individual demand can only be of 0 or 1, the total demand for a good is equal to the total number of consumers who ask for this good at given prices.

We now consider the supply side. There are two firms: firm A produces good A and firm B, good B. Each firm, whether A or B, must incur a sunk fixed cost,[5] I_A or I_B, and a unit cost, c_A or c_B, with $c_A < a + \eta$ and $c_B < b$. Total costs are thus given by $I_A + c_A d_A$ and $I_B + c_B d_B$.

What happens when both I_A and I_B are equal to zero? Each firm will then make a profit by selling any positive amount of its product at a price greater than unit cost. Together, these two firms constitute a duopoly with vertical differentiation. The differentiation is called vertical because, if the price for both goods is identical, all consumers buy good A. If, moreover, unit costs are such that $a - c_A \geqslant b - c_B$, not only can firm A provide a higher quality product, but also, it can

---

[5] However small the quantity of good A produced, firm A must incur the cost I_A (I_A is a fixed cost); moreover, in case of exit from the market, firm A has no possibility of recovering even a fraction of I_A (I_A is a sunk cost); the same is of course true of I_B.

profitably sell good A at a price such that all consumers will purchase it. Firm A is then a natural monopoly.[6] However, it is generally not in the best interest of firm A to set a price $p_A \leqslant a - b + c_B$ so as to attract all consumers away from firm B. Firm A will be better off selling at a higher price, even if this implies a loss of consumers to firm B. We shall thus examine how competition between A and B will lead to market-sharing, assuming that $a - c_A = b - c_B$, i.e. assuming the minimum advantage that still makes A a natural monopoly.

2. Entry versus Potential Competition

When sunk costs I_A and I_B are zero, there will be entry by both firms; more precisely, there is no specific entry decision: both firms are by nature in the market. On the other hand, competition is imperfect since there are only two firms competing and they behave strategically; that is, each firm takes the other firm's behaviour into account when deciding on its own behaviour (cf. the case with perfect competition, in Appendix A1). For example, when the prices are the decision variables, and p_A is firm A's price, a possible strategy for firm B is to choose the price p_B that maximizes its own profit given p_A. We shall refer to the outcome of this maximization problem as the best response of firm B to the price p_A. For any given price p_A,[7] there will be a best response $p_B(p_A)$, and we shall call this function the reaction function of firm B.

Formally, the best response $p_B(p_A)$ is the solution of the maximization problem

$$\max_{p_B} \pi_B(p_A, p_B) \tag{5.5}$$

where

$$\pi_B(p_A, p_B) = (p_B - c_B)d_B(p_A, p_B) \tag{5.6}$$

is firm B's profit. The reaction function $p_A(p_B)$ of firm A is defined in a similar way. In the model outlined in Section 1, the reaction functions are linear,[8] as is immediately seen by solving (5.5).

[6] For a survey of the various approaches to the natural monopoly, see Waterson (1987).

[7] We take for granted that firm·A will never set a price smaller than c_A nor a price above $a + \eta$. Outside of this range, firm A would either make losses or sell nothing.

[8] See Figure 5.2, which depicts a case where $\eta \geqslant a - c_A$.

We shall look at two forms of competition in prices,[9] which lead to two different equilibria; in both cases, éach firm's share of the market and profit depend on the prices set by the two of them. To begin with, we shall assume that both firms choose prices simultaneously. This leads to a Bertrand–Nash equilibrium.[10] Later on, we shall assume that one firm moves first by setting its price before the other firm decides on its own. This leads to a Stackelberg equilibrium in prices.

A Bertrand equilibrium corresponds to a form of competition where both firms act as follows: each firm chooses its price so as to maximize profits given the other firm's price. An equilibrium is reached when neither firm wants to change its price, given the price of the other firm. In other words, (p_A^*, p_B^*) is a Bertrand equilibrium if the best response of firm B to price p_A^* is p_B^*, i.e. if $p_B^* = p_B(p_A^*)$, and, vice versa if the best response of firm A to price p_B^* is p_A^*, i.e. if $p_A^* = p_A(p_B^*)$.

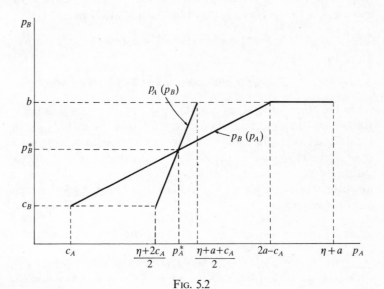

FIG. 5.2

[9] I.e. of imperfect competition with the prices as decision variables.

[10] Named after J. Bertrand, 'Commentaire à propos des "Recherches sur les principes mathématiques de la théorie des richesses"', *Journal des Savants*, 1883. Bertrand equilibrium is a particular variety of the more general Nash equilibrium; for an introduction to the concepts of game theory that are of common use in economics, see Moulin (1982).

In the market that we are considering here, there exists a unique Bertrand equilibrium (p_A^*, p_B^*), which is the unique intersection point of the two reaction functions (see Figure 5.2), namely:

(i) if $\eta \leqslant 3(b - c_B)$,
$$p_A^* = c_A + \tfrac{2}{3}\eta \quad \text{and} \quad p_B^* = c_B + \tfrac{1}{3}\eta;$$

(ii) if $\eta \geqslant 3(b - c_B)$,
$$p_A^* = p_A^m \quad \text{and} \quad p_B^* = p_B^m;$$

with
$$p_A^m = \tfrac{1}{2}(\eta + a + c_A) \quad \text{and} \quad p_B^m = b.$$

p_A^m is the monopoly price that A sets when it does not face any competition, i.e. when it is an unconstrained monopoly;[11] in the same way, p_B^m is B's monopoly price.

When $\eta \leqslant 3(b - c_B)$, there will be active competition between both firms since each has to take account of the other's presence in the market. Their respective shares of the market are then
$$d_A^* = d_A(p_A^*, p_B^*) = \tfrac{2}{3}l \quad \text{and} \quad d_B^* = d_B(p_A^*, p_B^*) = \tfrac{1}{3}l.$$
The corresponding profits are
$$\pi_A^* = \pi_A(p_A^*, p_B^*) = \tfrac{4}{9}l\eta \quad \text{and} \quad \pi_B^* = \pi_A(p_A^*, p_B^*) = \tfrac{1}{9}l\eta.$$

On the other hand, when $\eta \geqslant 3(b - c_B)$, firm A is in a position to set the monopoly price that would prevail if firm B were not around. Firm B then serves the customers who are disregarded by firm A. We shall refer to this case as to the double monopoly case. Firm A is indifferent to the presence of firm B when B charges $p_B = b$; indeed, in this case consumers get no more utility from buying good B than from not buying it.

---

[11] When A is alone serving the market $[0, l]$, the demand for good A is $d_A^m(p_A)$, as given by (5.3). A's profit is then
$$\pi_A^m(p_A) = (p_A - c_A)d_A^m(p_A).$$
When, moreover, A is an unconstrained monopoly, it chooses p_A so to maximize its profit:
$$\max_{p_A} \pi_A^m(p_A).$$
The solution of the maximization problem is the monopoly price p_A^m, with
$$p_A^m = \frac{1}{2}(\eta + a + c_A) \qquad \text{if } \eta \geqslant a - c_A$$
$$p_A^m = a \qquad \text{if } \eta \leqslant a - c_A.$$

As mentioned earlier, a Stackelberg equilibrium[12] corresponds to another form of competition. One firm, say A, plays the role of leader in choosing prices, and B plays the role of follower: firm B still chooses its profit-maximizing price given firm A's price, whereas firm A chooses its profit-maximizing price given firm B's reaction function, and not given B's price.[13] In other words, (p_A^s, p_B^s) is a Stackelberg equilibrium in prices if p_A^s is a solution of

$$\max_{p_A} \pi_A \{p_A, p_B(p_A)\}$$

and if

$$p_B^s = p_B(p_A^s).$$

In our particular model, there exists a unique Stackelberg equilibrium, namely:

(i) if $\eta \leqslant 2(b - c_B)$

$$p_A^s = c_A + \eta \quad \text{and} \quad p_B^s = c_B + \tfrac{1}{2}\eta;$$

(ii) If $2(b - c_B) \leqslant \eta \leqslant 3(b - c_B)$,

$$p_A^s = c_A + 2(b - c_B) \quad \text{and} \quad p_B^s = b;$$

(iii) if $3(b - c_B) \leqslant \eta$,

$$p_A^s = \tfrac{1}{2}(\eta + a + c_A) \quad \text{and} \quad p_B^s = b.$$

At the Stackelberg equilibrium, competition is less intense and thus less favourable to the consumers than at the Bertrand equilibrium: the prices and profits are higher for B as well as for A. Consider, for instance, the case where $\eta \leqslant 2(b - c_B)$. Then the respective market shares are

$$d_A^s = d_A(p_A^s, p_B^s) = \tfrac{1}{2}l \quad \text{and} \quad d_B^s = d_B(p_A^s, p_B^s) = \tfrac{1}{2}l.$$

The fact that firm A's demand d_A^s is less than d_A^* is more than compensated for, in terms of profit, by the increase in price from p_A^* to p_A^s. The profits at the Stackelberg equilibrium indeed are

$$\pi_A^s = \pi_A(p_A^s, p_B^s) = \tfrac{1}{2}l\eta \quad \text{and} \quad \pi_B^s = \pi_B(p_A^s, p_B^s) = \tfrac{1}{4}l\eta.$$

The above discussion suggests that consumers are better off when the two firms compete than when A is an unconstrained monopoly; and they are all the better as the competition between firms is more intense. It would however be more efficient to have only firm A

---

[12] Named after H. von Stackelberg, in *Marktform und Gleichgewicht*, 1934.

[13] If one inverted the role of both firms, there would be a Stackelberg equilibrium led by B whose existence conditions, in the market we have here, are similar.

operating since it is a natural monopoly. This raises the question of whether firm A's price can be lowered, at least to the level prevailing under active competition, without firm B entering the market. In other words, can potential competition function and be more efficient than active competition?

To address this question we must now describe the effects of potential competition; that is, how would the threat of entry by firm B discipline firm A's pricing behaviour? We thus have the following situation: firm A is in the market, whereas firm B is a potential entrant. Firm A, having already sunk its fixed cost of entry I_A, now behaves as if it were incurring only a unit cost c_A. On the other hand firm B, not having yet entered the market, has not yet spent anything. If I_B is zero—this being a limit case—there is no entry decision: B meets the consumers' demand without having to make a prior decision about entry. If I_B is positive, B must first decide whether or not to enter, i.e. must decide whether or not to sink the cost I_B. When B has entered, if it decides to, then both fixed costs have been sunk and it is as if there were no fixed costs at all; we are back to the previous analysis of active competition.

Let us therefore examine firm B as it is considering entering the market. It must form conjectures about firm A's response to its entry decision. Is post-entry price competition going to result in a Bertrand equilibrium, or in a Stackelberg equilibrium, or in some other outcome? Assuming that post-entry competition results in a Bertrand equilibrium outcome, firm B's profit will be π_B^*, in which case it will be profitable for B to enter if and only if $I_B < \pi_B^*$.[14] If, on the other hand, firm B assumes that post-entry competition results in a Stackelberg equilibrium, it must compare I_B to π_B^s.

Let us consider the first hypothesis. B thinks that post-entry competition results in a Bertrand equilibrium. Firm B will therefore not enter the market if $I_B \geqslant \pi_B^*$. B's decision does not depend on whether A profits little or much by its present monopoly position. From firm B's perspective, if B decides to enter the market, A will then, and only then, take B's price into account and accordingly will fix the price for its own good; similarly, B will take A's response into account, ..., and all this will generate a Bertrand equilibrium.

Implicit in the above line of argument is the assumption that firm

[14] For expository purposes we shall assume that, if $I_B = \pi_B^*$, then firm B will not enter the market.

A's price is flexible. Even if firm A were able to commit itself not to lower its price in response to firm B's entry, it would not want to do so since that could only make entry more attractive to firm B. We shall later examine the extent to which a public authority might wish to alter firm A's behaviour. In the absence of any such authority, the outcome of this game is straightforward: A behaves as an unconstrained monopoly as long as there is no entry by firm B; furthermore, because post-entry competition resulting in a Bertrand equilibrium is a sufficient deterrent, there is actually no entry.

On the other hand, if $I_B < \pi_B^*$, firm B will enter unless firm A takes some actions to reduce firm B's post-entry profit, by a sufficient amount to make entry unattractive. Firm A can deter entry in this way only if it can commit itself to a post-entry price, and if this price is lower than the Bertrand equilibrium price. Such a post-entry commitment usually involves a commitment to an identical pre-entry price. For example, a typical form of commitment is to sign a binding contract with customers; usually the price agreed upon in such a contract cannot be made contingent on the event of entry. The same is true for a commitment guaranteed by a public authority. Hence we take for granted that, when firm A commits itself to a price, the commitment is binding whether firm B enters the market or not.

Assuming that such commitments are feasible, firm A may choose between two lines of action:

1. to commit itself to a price that will indeed deter entry;
2. to commit itself to the Stackelberg price, which will provoke entry, albeit with a result that is better for both firms than the Bertrand equilibrium.

Firm A will choose according to whether it can have a higher profit by deterring entry or by inducing the Stackelberg equilibrium. Let us now see how these profits compare.

We know that, if firm A chooses $p_A = p_A^*$, the response of firm B is $p_B(p_A^*) = p_B^*$, bringing B the profit

$$\pi_B\{p_A^*, p_B(p_A^*)\} = \pi_B^* > I_B.$$

If, alternatively, A chooses the lowest possible price, i.e. $p_A = c_A$, the response of B is $p_B(c_A)$, bringing B the profit

$$\pi_B\{c_A, p_B(c_A)\} = 0 \leqslant I_B.$$

Since $\pi_B\{p_A, p_B(p_A)\}$ is a continuous function and is increasing in p_A, there exists a unique price p_A^d between c_A and p_A^*, such that

$$\pi_B\{p_A^d, p_B(p_A^d)\} = I_B. \tag{5.7}$$

This price p_A^d is the highest price that A can set and still deter entry by B. A then remains the only firm in the market and its profit is

$$\pi_A^m(p_A^d) = (p_A^d - c_A) d_A^m(p_A^d).$$

It is in A's interest to set p_A^d and deter entry provided I_B is big enough, that is, provided it is possible to have (5.7) and at the same time to have

$$\pi_A^m(p_A^d) \geqslant \pi_A^s. \tag{5.8}$$

When $\eta \leqslant \frac{3}{2}(b - c_B)$,[15] (5.7) and (5.8) respectively read

$$\frac{l}{\eta}\left(\frac{p_A^d - c_A}{2}\right)^2 = I_B \tag{5.7'}$$

$$(p_A^d - c_A)l \geqslant \frac{l\eta}{2} \tag{5.8'}$$

These two conditions will be simultaneously satisfied if

$$I_B \geqslant \frac{l\eta}{16} = \tfrac{9}{16}\pi_B^*.$$

There is thus a critical value I_B^c of I_B, which is equal to $\frac{9}{16}\pi_B^*$ in the case where $\eta \leqslant \frac{3}{2}(b - c_B)$.[16] If I_B is greater than I_B^c, A is better off fixing the price p_A^d to deter B from entering. If I_B is smaller than I_B^c, A is better off fixing the price p_A^s, thus provoking the entry of B, albeit in relatively good conditions from A's point of view.

Thus, in the absence of any intervention from a public authority, the following outcomes may occur:

1. If $I_B \geqslant \pi_B^*$, then firm A is alone in the market and faces no threat of entry; A is an unconstrained monopoly and sets the price p_A^m.
2. If $I_B < \pi_B^*$, then either A is unable to commit itself to a particular price, in which case the Bertrand equilibrium will result, or it can commit itself to a price, in which case there are two possibilities:

---

[15] We focus on this case because the condition $\eta \leqslant \frac{3}{2}(b - c_B)$ implies that $d_A^m(p_A^d) = l$; (5.8) then reduces to a particularly simple expression.

[16] This critical value is the same for $\frac{3}{2}(b - c_B) \leqslant \eta \leqslant 2(b - c_B)$. If $2(b - c_B) \leqslant \eta \leqslant 3(b - c_B)$, then

$$I_B^c = \frac{9}{4}\left(1 - \frac{b - c_B}{\eta}\right)^2 \pi_B^*.$$

If $3(b - c_B) \leqslant \eta$, we know that A is in a monopoly position despite the presence of B.

(a) if $I_B^c \leqslant I_B$, A will commit itself to the price p_A^d and prevent entry by firm B; we refer to this situation as firm A being disciplined by the potential competition from firm B; A is a constrained monopoly;

(b) if $I_B < I_B^c$, A will commit itself to the price p_A^s; B enters and the Stackelberg equilibrium obtains.

The threat of entry by a potential competitor brings about welfare improvements for two reasons. First, potential rather than active competition avoids unnecessary duplication. Second, to deter entry by firm B, firm A must commit itself to a price not only below the monopoly price p_A^m, but also below the Bertrand equilibrium price p_A^*. Thus, potential competition leads to better terms of trade for the consumers than would be obtained under active competition.[17]

When $I_B \geqslant \pi_B^*$, firm B's entry is blockaded and firm A will behave without regard to any entry threat. It will charge the monopoly price p_A^m; this moreover may result in part of the market not being served. On the other hand, when $I_B < I_B^c$, and assuming that firm A can commit itself to a price, entry will be accommodated and competition will be soft, with A and B setting the Stackelberg prices p_A^s and p_B^s. How could a public authority improve these situations in the interest of the consumers, assuming that it can identify whether $I_B \geqslant \pi_B^*$ or $I_B < I_B^c$?

3. Public Policies for Promoting Potential Competition

When $I_B < I_B^c$, and there is no public intervention, the outcome is the Stackelberg equilibrium if firm A can commit itself to a price, the Bertrand equilibrium otherwise. This situation can be changed by raising I_B above I_B^c. To do so, the public authority might announce that it will tax, at a suitable rate, investments aimed at extending the capacity to serve the market considered. Then firm B must spend more than I_B^c to enter the market, and firm A, if it can commit itself to a price, finds it in its best interest to deter entry. No tax is actually levied, and potential competition prevails.

When $I_B \geqslant \pi_B^*$, and when there is no public intervention, firm A is an unconstrained monopoly; the expected outcome of post-entry

[17] Note however that entry by firm B may be preferable for those consumers whose preference for good A is only slightly greater than for good B; the lower p_A^d is, the less significant is this effect.

competition deters firm B from entering. Here, lowering I_B beneath π_B^* would be appropriate. To do so, the public authority might announce that it will subsidize, at a suitable rate, investments in the market. Then firm B can spend less than π_B^* to enter the market, which it does if firm A does not change its behaviour. Here again, owing to the public intervention, firm A finds it in its best interest to deter entry, provided it can commit itself to a price. No subsidy must actually be paid, and potential competition prevails.

In both cases, of course, the public authority should not erode the commitment possibilities of firm A. It might instead want to facilitate or even impose commitment.

The above discussion clearly indicates that very different policies are required depending on whether I_B is high ($I_B \geqslant \pi_B^*$) or low ($I_B < I_B^c$). To further illustrate how important it is that public policies be correctly directed, taking into account the relevant features of the market, consider the following simple extension of the model. Suppose that consumers are now represented by points in a rectangle of length l and height h. A priori, this looks like an innocuous modification of the model; the density of consumers per unit length is now h instead of 1. This does not affect equilibrium prices and simply increases demand by a factor h. Thus, Bertrand equilibrium prices are still given by

$$p_A^* = c_A + \tfrac{2}{3}\,\eta. \quad \text{and} \quad p_B^* = c_B + \tfrac{1}{3}\eta.$$

The corresponding equilibrium demands are

$$d_A^* = \tfrac{2}{3}hl \quad \text{and} \quad d_B^* = \tfrac{1}{3}hl.$$

However, this seemingly uninteresting generalization of the representation of consumers allows us to introduce other forms of competition than those considered so far. Indeed, firm B may be better off serving less than d_B^* if this comes along with a price that is sufficiently higher than p_B^* to compensate for the corresponding reduction in sales. To this end, B may consider restricting its custom *a priori*,[18] i.e. before the market starts functioning. It can implement such a voluntary reduction in sales opportunities through various methods, such as restricting the extension of its distribution network, or targeting its advertising to a restricted category of customers.

Consider for example that firm B *a priori* restricts its custom in

---

[18] This creates a discrimination between consumers; for a discussion of various forms of discrimination, see ch. 6.

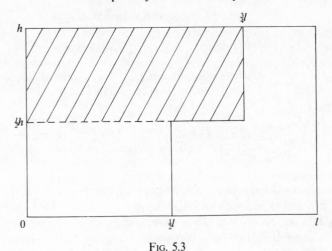

FIG. 5.3

such a way that it will not serve, whatever the prevailing prices, any customer in the subset represented by the shaded rectangle in Figure 5.3; the length and height of this rectangle are, respectively, $\frac{3}{4}l$ and $\frac{1}{2}h$. This subset of customers is thus a captive market for firm A. However, since firm A sets the same price in this captive market as in the market where it faces the competition of firm B, its price decision in the captive market will be constrained by competition in the contestable market. This situation results in a restricted Bertrand equilibrium, with prices

$$\tilde{p}_A = c_A + \tfrac{5}{4}\eta \quad \text{and} \quad \tilde{p}_B = c_B + \tfrac{3}{4}\eta,$$

and with demands (see Figure 5.3)

$$\tilde{d}_A = \tfrac{5}{8}hl \quad \text{and} \quad \tilde{d}_B = \tfrac{3}{8}hl$$

and profits

$$\tilde{\pi}_A = \tfrac{25}{32}hl\eta \quad \text{and} \quad \tilde{\pi}_B = \tfrac{9}{32}hl\eta.$$

This equilibrium outcome is intermediate between two polar cases: the (unrestricted) Bertrand equilibrium outcome, and the double monopoly outcome.

The restricted Bertrand equilibrium brings about higher profits than the Bertrand equilibrium. Competition between firms is softened, and they extract more of the consumers' surplus. Whether the public authority should oppose firm B's restrictive practices, however, is not obvious, since this restricted form of active competition

TABLE 5.1. Restricting competition

Range of I_B	Unrestricted	Restricted
$I_B \geqslant \tilde{\pi}_B$	Unconstrained monopoly	Unconstrained monopoly
$\tilde{\pi}_B > I_B \geqslant \tilde{I}_B^c$	Unconstrained monopoly	Potential competition
$\tilde{I}_B^c > I_B \geqslant \pi_B^*$	Unconstrained monopoly	Restricted Bertrand equil.
$\pi_B^* > I_B \geqslant I_B^c$	Potential competition	Restricted Bertrand equil.
$I_B^c > I_B \geqslant 0$	Stackelberg equil.	Restricted Bertrand equil.

may enhance the prospects of potential competition. Table 5.1 shows the results obtained with and without restriction, for various values of I_B taking into account the prospects of potential competition.

The table indicates that the set of values of I_B that result in potential competition when there is no restriction is disjoint from the set of similar values when there is restriction. For example, for high values of I_B, still below $\tilde{\pi}_B$, restricted competition in the post-entry game is sufficiently soft to induce entry unless firm A commits itself to an entry-deterring price, which in fact it is in its best interest to do. When unrestricted, on the other hand, post-entry competition is tough enough to deter entry for the same values of I_B; there is no entry threat from firm B, and firm A is an unconstrained monopoly. Now consider low values of I_B, specifically, values between I_B^c and π_B^*. In this range firm A takes actions to deter entry when post-entry competition is unrestricted; but A prefers restricted competition to deterrence, in which case the benefits of potential competition are lost.

To summarize, this simple extension of the basic model clearly illustrates that public policy must properly take into account the characteristics of the market and the expected forms of post-entry competition in so far as they influence, in a decisive but diverse manner, the prospects of potential competition. Such consideration must, for instance, guide the public authority in its reaction to restrictive practices such as those adopted here by firm B. At first sight, it would seem that the public authority should oppose such restrictive practices. The above analysis leads to more qualified conclusions: the restrictive practices may facilitate firm B's entry and therefore increase the threat that such entry represents for firm A. Hence they widen the span of potential competition. This being in the interest of the consumers, the public authority should avoid putting obstacles in the way. On the other hand, it should take appropriate measures when the restrictive practices, instead of promoting potential competition, lead to a soft form of active competition which unduly favours the firms to the detriment of the consumers.

6

Discrimination in the Public Interest

1. Making Good Use of Discrimination in Public Services

In 1875, the government of the Canton de Vaud—one of the states in the Swiss Confederation—discussed the advisability of buying out the railways operated in the canton by private companies. They asked Léon Walras, then professor of economics at Lausanne University, for advice. Walras took the matter very seriously and produced a long memoire,[1] in which he applied his theoretical insight to a broad range of empirical data.

How the companies discriminate between their customers is one of the points that Walras considered at some length. Self-selection devices, he remarked, are used on a large scale by the companies to discriminate:

The companies consider, rightly or wrongly, the average price of 7.66c to be the profit-maximising price; but they do not want to miss the chance of taking more from passengers willing to pay more, nor to turn away passengers not willing to pay as much. This is why there are three separate classes, and great efforts made to accentuate on the one hand the advantages of the first class and on the other the disadvantages of the third class. When some time ago there was an outcry that third class coaches should have windows fitted as laid down in the regulations for 1857–8, and now when heating is demanded for them in the winter, people complain about the meanness of the companies without understanding its true cause. If the third class coaches were comfortable enough for many first and second class passengers to go in them, total net product would fall. That is all there is to it. The companies only have third class coaches to avoid losing a large number of less well off passengers who would rather go by stage coach than pay the first or second class fare.

Walras makes it clear that the reason why the companies discriminate is simply that discriminating increases their profits. Nowhere in

---

[1] *L'Etat et les chemins de fer*, translated in Holmes (1980).

his memoire does he consider what the attitude of public companies, pursuing other goals than mere profit-seeking, should be with respect to price and quality discrimination. Is discrimination exclusively geared to profit-seeking, or could it also be used, in certain circumstances, to increase the welfare of the customers? To answer this question, let us consider two cities which are separated by a sea channel. Between them, two means of transport are available. One is free, but slow. The other is rapid, but costly; the trip takes t fewer hours, but a fixed cost C must be supported.[2] The responsibility for this second means is granted to a public firm, which is not allowed to make a profit but must cover the cost through its receipts. If the firm uses a single price p—so that any traveller using this means must pay p—balancing cost and receipts requires

$$N(p)p = C$$

where $N(p)$ designates the number of travellers adopting the rapid means of transport when its price is p.

What are the determinants of $N(p)$? There are two types of travellers:[3] for type 1, each hour gained during the trip is worth q_1, and for type 2 it is worth only $q_2 < q_1$. Since the slow trip lasts t more hours than the fast one, a type 1 traveller is ready to adopt the more rapid means if its price is not greater than $\bar{p}_1 = tq_1$. Similarly, a type 2 traveller will adopt the more rapid means only if the price is not greater than $\bar{p}_2 = tq_2 < \bar{p}_1$. As a result,

$$
\begin{array}{lll}
\text{if } p \leqslant \bar{p}_2 & \quad & N(p) = N_1 + N_2 \\
\text{if } \bar{p}_2 < p \leqslant \bar{p}_1 & \quad & N(p) = N_1 \\
\text{if } \bar{p}_1 < p & \quad & N(p) = 0
\end{array}
$$

where N_1 and N_2 are the respective memberships of the two types.

We are interested in those situations where $\bar{p}_1$ and $\bar{p}_2$ are sufficiently different so that

$$N_1 \bar{p}_1 > C \tag{6.1}$$

and yet,

$$(N_1 + N_2)\bar{p}_2 < C. \tag{6.2}$$

---

[2] For a more general cost structure, see Henriet *et al.* (1988).

[3] We consider that they cannot abstain from travelling, but can only choose which means of transport to use. We are thus considering a good of which each consumer uses just one unit, whose quality can vary. Considering on the other hand a good whose quality remains fixed but for which the quantity demanded can vary from one consumer to another, L. Phlips shows how a nonlinear price schedule can be a discriminatory instrument favourable for all concerned parties (Phlips, 1983, ch. 10).

Assumption (6.1) means that type 1 travellers are prepared to pay a price that is sufficiently high to cover the fixed cost of the rapid service. Assumption (6.2) means that this cost cannot be covered through the setting of a price acceptable to type 2 travellers. As a result, it seems that the public firm is forced to set the price $p = C/N_1$, which excludes type 2 from the rapid service and makes type 1 carry the whole weight of financing C.

Were it possible for the firm to know at a glance to which type a traveller belongs, it could use a discriminatory price schedule, charging each type a different price. For the moment, however, we will consider that such authoritarian discrimination is not possible. Could we then imagine a voluntary discrimination, or self-selection, by permitting all travellers to choose between two prices, but arranging that each price will be chosen by the type for which it is intended? This is of course not possible if the same service is provided for everyone, but perhaps it is possible if different services are proposed. For example, the rapid means of transport may offer services at two speeds, one of which is slower than the best possible service.[4]

Let us explore this suggestion, which at first glance looks rather strange:

— at a price p_1, the traveller has the right to a (true) rapid service, which saves him t hours compared to the slow means of transport; the latter is still free of charge;
— at a price $p_2 < p_1$, the traveller has the right to a debased rapid service, which saves him only $t - s$ hours compared with the slow means of transport ($0 < s < t$).

Because of (6.2), the budget balance of the firm requires that $p_1 > \bar{p}_2$. How will travellers make their choice? If p_2 is too big and $t - s$ too small, type 2 travellers will not choose $(p_2, t - s)$, but will continue to use the slow means of transport. They will choose $(p_2, t - s)$ if and only if

$$(t - s)q_2 \geqslant p_2$$

[4] For example, by voluntarily lengthening boarding times, however ridiculous this idea seems at first glance. Table 6.1 shows a more realistic example of a restriction coming along with a reduced fare offered by Air France and British Airways: a return ticket London–Paris–London in economy class without any restriction of use (Y) costs £170 (UKL), while the same ticket, but for the 'Sunday rule' (Y PX/SU), costs £86.

TABLE 6.1. From IATA/EUROPE passenger tariff

	LONPAR	APR 88	UKL
Y		85	170
Y	PX/SU*	—	86

*SU return rule means: return travel from the last stopover point outside the country of origin shall not be commenced prior 00.01h on the Sunday following the date of international departure from the country of point of origin.

or, equivalently,

$$s \leqslant \phi(p_2),$$

with

$$\phi(p_2) = \frac{\bar{p}_2 - p_2}{q_2}. \tag{6.3}$$

$\phi(p_2)$ designates the maximum reduction in speed that type 2 travellers are ready to accept along with the price p_2. If the reduction is more that $\phi(p_2)$, they do not think it worth while to pay p_2 and prefer the slow means. On the other hand, if $p_1 - p_2$ is too big considering the size of s, the reduction in speed s will not deter type 1 travellers from choosing $(p_2, t - s)$. Indeed, they will choose (p_1, t) if and only if

$$sq_1 \geqslant p_1 - p_2$$

or, equivalently,

$$s \geqslant \Psi(p_1, p_2),$$

with

$$\Psi(p_1, p_2) = \frac{p_1 - p_2}{q_1}. \tag{6.4}$$

$\Psi(p_1, p_2)$ designates the minimum reduction in speed still inducing type 1 travellers to pay the supplement in price $p_1 - p_2$ and choose the (true) rapid service.

Let us suppose that p_1, p_2 and s are such that the first type does choose (p_1, t), the second type $(p_2, t - s)$, and that these choices are compatible with the budget balance of the public firm. The following conditions are thus satisfied simultaneously:

$$N_1 p_1 + N_2 p_2 = C \tag{6.5}$$

and

$$\Psi(p_1, p_2) \leqslant s \leqslant \phi(p_2). \tag{6.6}$$

Is this possible? Is it of any interest?

To answer the first question, let us compare the two functions $\phi(p_2)$ and $\Psi\{p_1(p_2), p_2\}$, where

$$p_1(p_2) = \frac{C - N_2 p_2}{N_1} \tag{6.7}$$

expresses the fact that the budget constraint (6.5) is satisfied, so that

$$\Psi\{p_1(p_2), p_2\} = \frac{C - (N_1 + N_2)p_2}{N_1 q_1}. \tag{6.8}$$

It is possible to satisfy simultaneously (6.5) and (6.6) if the two straight lines $\phi(p_2)$ and $\Psi\{p_1(p_2), p_2\}$ intersect between $p_2 = 0$ and $p_2 = \bar{p}_2$ (see Figure 6.1), i.e. if

$$\phi(0) \geqslant \Psi\{p_1(0), 0\}$$

or

$$t \geqslant \frac{C}{Nq_1}.$$

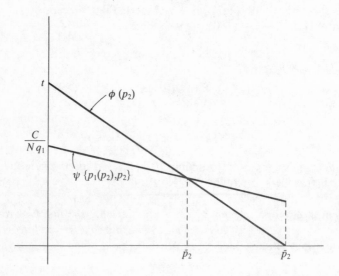

Fig. 6.1

The latter condition is fulfilled because of (6.1). Hence there exists between 0 and $\bar{p}_2$ a price $\tilde{p}_2$ such that

$$\phi(\tilde{p}_2) = \Psi\{p_1(\tilde{p}_2), \tilde{p}_2\}$$

and, for each p_2 with $0 \leqslant p_2 < \tilde{p}_2$,

$$\phi(p_2) > \Psi\{p_1(p_2), p_2\}.$$

Let, for such p_2,

$$s(p_2) = \Psi\{p_1(p_2), p_2\} \tag{6.9}$$

be the smallest reduction in speed compatible with the necessity to prevent type 1 travellers from choosing $(p_2, t - s)$.

The interest in having (6.5) and (6.6) satisfied simultaneously is now clear. It permits a choice of p_2, p_1, and s—namely $p_2 < \tilde{p}_2$, $p_1 = p_1(p_2)$, and $s = s(p_2)$—so that there is a self-selection which is both compatible with the budget balance of the public firm and advantageous for both types of users. In fact, in relation to the situation where they alone use the rapid means of transport, type 1 travellers pay less for the same service,[5] while type 2 travellers pay, for an intermediate quality of service, a price sufficiently advantageous that they prefer this service to the slow means of transport. The choice $s = s(p_2)$ reduces to a minimum the waste represented by the reduction in speed of the rapid means of transport, a minimum that is unavoidable if the mechanism of self-selection is to work. The offer of both $\{p_2, t - s(p_2)\}$ and $\{p_1(p_2), t\}$ is thus optimal in the sense that it induces the realization of an allocation that is a second-best Pareto optimum in this economic situation where no authoritarian discrimination is possible but where there is no restriction on the operation of self-selection. The greater p_2 is in the interval $[0, \tilde{p}_2]$, the better for type 1 is the optimum, and inversely for type 2.

Let us now consider the case where it is possible to identify at a glance some users belonging to the second type; they have a specific

---

[5] Unless $p_2 = 0$, in which case p_1 stays equal to C/N_1. If the firm, instead of seeking a Pareto optimum through self-selection s.t. the budget constraint, would seek to maximize its profit, it would choose s not according to (6.9), but according to $s = \phi(p_2)$. This would permit the firm to maximize p_1 for a given p_2, and hence to maximize its profit for a given p_2 while still fulfilling (6.6). It would then maximize its profit in p_2. Owing to the linearity in this model, this maximization would lead the firm to fix $p_1 = \bar{p}_1, p_2 = 0$, and $s = t$, that is to depend on the first type of users alone, at the highest price possible. However, this last result depends on the peculiarities of the model. It is just one possible case, as S. Salop's *Noisy Monopolist* shows (Salop 1977).

trait a,[6] which is easily verified and difficult to fake. To these users, numbering $N_2^a < N_2$, the public firm may offer the price p_2 without the reduction $s(p_2)$ in speed. There is no danger of granting the benefit of this special offer to type 1 users by mistake, since by definition there is no problem of identification. Actually, these type 2 users with trait a may also be made to pay a price π^a different from p_2, as long as this price is not greater than a threshold beyond which they would prefer to accept the debased service normally imposed with price p_2.

We can, through this combination of segmentation[7] and self-selection, improve for all the users the optima previously obtained through self-selection alone. Let us consider an offer $\{p_2, t - s(p_2)\}$ and $\{p_1(p_2), t\}$ corresponding to one of these optima and try to improve it through the following modifications:

— The price $p_1(p_2)$ is lowered: the rapid service is offered (to all users) at a price π_1 such that

$$\bar{p}_2 < \pi_1 < p_1(p_2).$$

— The reduction in speed $s(p_2)$ is diminished accordingly: $s(p_2)$ is replaced by

$$\sigma = \frac{\pi_1 - p_2}{q_2}.$$

— To the users of type 2 having trait a, and only to them, the rapid service is offered at a price π^a such that

$$p_2 < \pi^a < \pi_1.$$

Can these modifications be implemented, and do they create an improvement for all users? They can be implemented if the budget balance of the public firm is assured, that is if

$$N_1 \pi_1 + N_2^a \pi^a + (N_2 - N_2^a)p_2 = C, \qquad (6.10)$$

and if type 2 users with trait a choose (π^a, t), that is if

$$\pi^a - p_2 \leqslant q_2 \sigma. \qquad (6.11)$$

Conditions (6.10) and (6.11) simply require that π_1 be not too much

---

[6] For instance, a can be 'having less than x years', 'having more than x years', or 'being married and accompanied by spouse', etc.

[7] The word 'segmentation' is used here in the sense of authoritarian discrimination, an option being reserved exclusively to a certain category of people; these also have access to the options that are open to the other categories.

lower than $p_1(p_2)$, namely,

$$p_1(p_2) - \pi_1 \leqslant \{p_1(p_2) - p_2\} \frac{N_2^a}{N_1 + N_2^a}. \tag{6.12}$$

Subject to (6.12), the proposed modifications—made possible by the interaction between segmentation and self-selection—constitute an improvement for all the users: those of type 1 receive the same service for a lower price, since $\pi_1 < p_1(p_2)$; those of type 2 not having trait a receive better service, since $\sigma < s(p_2)$, at a price that remains unchanged; and finally, those of type 2 having trait a receive the best service, at a price that is attractive to them, since $\pi^a - p_2 < q_2\sigma$.

However, it is rare that type and trait fit as well as we have supposed up to now. In general, there are also N_1^a users of type 1 who have trait a. In some cases, the segmentation plainly cannot be put into effect. It can be put into effect to the benefit of all the users if there exists between p_2 and $\bar{p}_2$ at least one π^a such that

$$(N_1 - N_1^a)p_1(p_2) + (N_1^a + N_2^a)\pi^a + (N_2 - N_2^a)p_2 = C \tag{6.13}$$

and

$$\pi^a - p_2 \leqslant q_2 s(p_2). \tag{6.14}$$

Eliminating π^a between (6.13) and (6.14), we obtain, after some algebraic manipulations, the condition

$$\frac{N_1^a}{N_1^a + N_2^a} \leqslant \frac{q_2}{q_1}. \tag{6.15}$$

If, and only if, this condition holds, there does exist at least one π^a between p_2 and $\bar{p}_2$ such that (6.13) and (6.14) are satisfied.

According to condition (6.15), N_1^a can be as much greater, relative to $N_1^a + N_2^a$, as q_2 is greater relative to q_1. This is not surprising since q_1 and q_2, absent in (6.13), appear in (6.14) solely through the ratio q_2/q_1; the right-hand side of (6.14) is indeed equal to $(q_2/q_1)\{p_1(p_2) - p_2\}$. Condition (6.14) is the less constraining the greater q_2/q_1 is; it is no surprise that the same is true for condition (6.15).[8]

***

[8] $N_1^a(N_1^a + N_2^a)^{-1}$ cannot, in any case, be greater than $N_1(N_1 + N_2)^{-1}$ since it results from (6.1) that $(q_2/q_1) < N_1(N_1 + N_2)^{-1}$.

Summing up, when the proportion of users of type 1 with trait a to the total of all users with trait a is not greater than q_2/q_1, using both segmentation and self-selection permits an improvement in the situation of all the users beyond that which is permitted by self-selection alone. This result seems natural if we observe that, the greater q_2 is, the more attractive it is for the N_2^a users of type 2 with trait a to avoid the reduction in speed, and hence the greater π^a can be. Also, the smaller q_1 is, the bigger s must be, to prevent users of type 1 without trait a from ceasing to use the rapid service. In this case, it is again more attractive for the same N_2^a users to avoid the reduction in speed.

All that precedes can easily be carried over to the more general case where the utility functions are no longer linear in the quality $x = t - s$ of service, in other words to the case where $(t - s)q_i$ is replaced by $v_i(t - s)$, v_i being an increasing, continuous, and concave function in $x = t - s$, with $v_i(0) = 0$ $(i = 1, 2)$. Under these circumstances, when faced with various pairs $(p, t - s)$, each composed of a price and a quality level, user i makes his choice by maximizing the utility function $v_i(t - s) - p$. We have already used this kind of additively separable utility function several times.

The conditions of self-selection become

$$v_2(t - s) \geqslant p_2,$$

which generalizes

$$(t - s)q_2 \geqslant p_2,$$

and also

$$v_1(t) - v_1(t - s) \geqslant p_1 - p_2,$$

which generalizes

$$sq_1 \geqslant p_1 - p_2.$$

Then

$$s = \phi(p_2)$$

is the solution of

$$v_2(t - s) = p_2,$$

and

$$s = \Psi(p_1, p_2)$$

is the solution of

$$v_1(t) - v_1(t - s) = p_1 - p_2.$$

We are thus driven to ask the same question as in the linear case: Does there exist p_1, p_2, and s for which we have simultaneously

$$N_1 p_1 + N_2 p_2 = C$$

and

$$\Psi(p_1, p_2) \leqslant s \leqslant \phi(p_2)?$$

In Figure 6.2, these conditions are satisfied with the prices p_1 and p_2 and any point on the segment DE. The equations of the curves OA_1, OA_2, and EB are, respectively, $p = v_1(t - s)$, $p = v_2(t - s)$, and $p = v_1(t - s) - \{v_1(t) - p_1\}$. Point E corresponds to a second-best Pareto optimum with self-selection. From there on, all of the results obtained in the linear case remain qualitatively true.

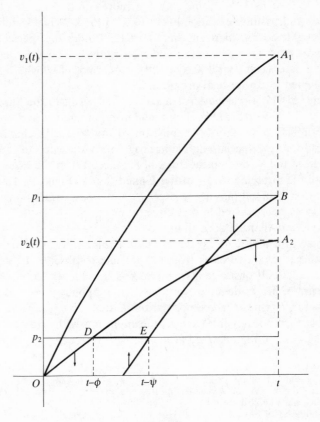

FIG. 6.2

2. Academic Performance and Professional Selection

'We granted certiorari to consider the important constitutional issue.' (Supreme Court of the United States, *Regents of the University of California* v. *Bakke*).

In 1973 Allan Bakke, a 'white male',[9] applied to the Medical School of the University of California at Davis. His application was considered by the 'general admissions program'. Despite a strong benchmark score of 468 out of 500, he was rejected. He applied again in 1974, and was again rejected. In both years, applicants were admitted under the 'special admissions program' with benchmark scores significantly lower than Bakke's. This special programme had been created in 1971 to increase the representation of 'disadvantaged' students in the school. From 1971 to 1974, 21 black students and 30 Mexican–Americans were admitted under the special programme, compared with only 1 and 6, respectively, under the general programme; each year 100 places were offerred, of which 16 were designated for the special programme.[10]

After his 1974 rejection, Allen Bakke filed a suit in the Superior Court of California. He sought 'mandatory, injunctive, and declaratory relief compelling his admission to the Medical School'. He alleged that the special admission programme 'operated to exclude him from the School on the basis of his race'. When the case came before the Supreme Court of the United States (Figure 6.3) it was clear that it raised important issues. Among these issues, some can profitably be discussed in economic terms.

Consider Allan Bakke's ability to be a successful medical student and, later on, a practitioner; let ω measure this ability. Although it is possible to conceive of ω, it is not possible to observe it directly. What is actually observed is Allan Bakke's 'benchmark score', i.e. the measure of his academic performance as an applicant; let y be this measure.[11] If, in the whole population of applicants, y is increasing with ω, then it is possible to select the applicants with greater ability on the basis of the observed academic performance.

---

[9] All the quotations are from *Regents of the University of California* v. *Bakke*. As for the judgment, it is reproduced here.

[10] In 1971–4, 12 Asians were also admitted under the special programme, and one place remained unfilled in 1971.

[11] For ease of exposition, we make the restrictive assumption that ability is intrinsic, hence does not depend on actions that might also affect y. See Spence (1974).

SUPREME COURT OF THE UNITED STATES

No. 76–811

Regents of the University of
California, Petitioner,
v.
Allan Bakke.

On Writ of Certiorari to the
Supreme Court of California.

[June 28, 1978]

MR JUSTICE POWELL announced the judgment of the Court.

This case presents a challenge to the special admissions program of the petitioner, the Medical School of the University of California at Davis, which is designed to assure the admission of a specified number of students from certain minority groups. The Superior Court of California sustained respondent's challenge, holding that petitioner's program violated the California Constitution, Title VI of the Civil Rights Act of 1964, 42 U.S.C. §2000d, and the Equal Protection Clause of the Fourteenth Amendment. The court enjoined petitioner from considering respondent's race or the race of any other applicant in making admissions decisions. It refused, however, to order respondent's admission to the Medical School, holding that he had not carried his burden of proving that he would have been admitted but for the constitutional and statutory violations. The Supreme Court of California affirmed those portions of the trial court's judgment declaring the special admissions program unlawful and enjoining petitioner from considering the race of any applicant.* It modified that portion of the judgment denying respondent's requested injunction and directed the trial court to order his admission.

For the reasons stated in the following opinion, I believe that so much of the judgment of the California court as holds petitioner's special admissions program unlawful and directs that respondent be admitted to the Medical School must be affirmed. For the reasons expressed in a separate opinion, my Brothers THE CHIEF JUSTICE, MR. JUSTICE STEWART, MR. JUSTICE REHNQUIST, and MR. JUSTICE STEVENS concur in this judgment.

I also conclude for the reasons stated in the following opinion that the portion of the court's judgment enjoining petitioner from according any consideration to race in its admissions process must be reversed. For reasons expressed in separate opinions, my Brothers MR. JUSTICE BRENNAN, MR. JUSTICE WHITE, MR. JUSTICE MARSHALL, and MR. JUSTICE BLACKMUN concur in this judgment.

Affirmed in part and reversed in part.

FIG. 6.3

This is no longer possible if the same academic performance may correspond to different abilities, as is the case with the applicants to the Davis Medical School, or with those depicted in Figures 6.4 and 6.5. Here the population of applicants is composed of two hetero-geneous sub-populations, A and B. The ability, $\omega(A)$, of an individual A^{12} is uniformly distributed in the interval $[\omega_2, \omega_1]$. His academic performance, $y(A)$, is also uniformly distributed, this time

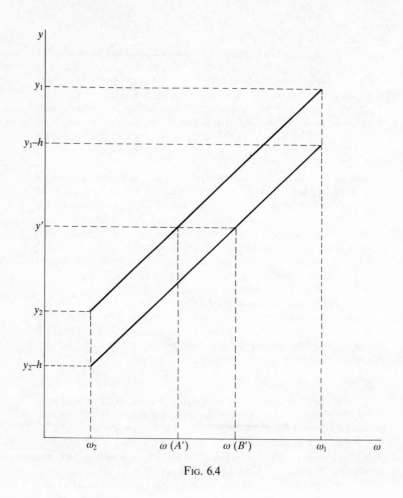

F*IG*. 6.4

---

[12] Shorthand for 'an individual in the sub-population A'.

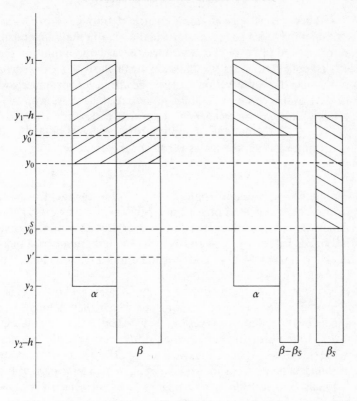

FIG. 6.5

in the interval $[y_2, y_1]$. The ability, $\omega(B)$, of an individual B is distributed in exactly the same way as $\omega(A)$ is: uniformly in $[\omega_2, \omega_1]$. As far as the academic performance is concerned, there is an important difference between the two sub-populations: $y(B)$ is uniformly distributed, albeit in the interval $[y_2 - h, y_1 - h]$. Sub-population B has a handicap h with respect to sub-population A as far as the production of academic performances is concerned. In each sub-population, academic performance increases with ability, but this is not true in the whole population; for instance, individual A', with ability $\omega(A')$, and individual B', with ability $\omega(B')$, produce the same academic performance y', $\omega(B')$ being none the less greater than $\omega(A')$.

If we knew the sub-population to which he belongs (A or B) and his academic performance, an individual would be fully identified. But this is not the case. To maximize the average ability of the selected applicants, when we thus can distinguish the individuals only through the observation of their academic performance, we must decide of a certain minimum y_0 and keep all those who self-select by achieving an academic performance superior to y_0. If, moreover, N_0 is the number of applicants to be selected ($N_0 = 100$ per year in the case of the Davis Medical School), we must fix y_0 so that

$$(y_1 - y_0)\alpha + (y_1 - h - y_0)\beta = N_0, \tag{6.16}$$

assuming that y_0 is smaller than $y_1 - h$. In (6.16), α is the density of individuals A at any level of academic performance between y_2 and y_1, and β is the density of individuals B at any level of academic performance between $y_2 - h$ and $y_1 - h$. The total number of individuals A is thus $(y_1 - y_2)\alpha$, and the total number of individuals B is $\{(y_1 - h) - (y_2 - h)\}\beta = (y_1 - y_2)\beta$.

How is the situation changed when, for some individuals at least, we know *a priori* the sub-population to which they belong? For example, by immediate observation, they can be held as individuals B. The population is then segmented[13] into two immediately discernible categories, whereas the two sub-populations are not directly discernible: category S (S for special) is composed of a part of the individuals B (density β_S), and category G (G for general) is composed of all the individuals A (density α) and all of the remaining individuals B (density $\beta - \beta_S$).

It then becomes possible to differentiate the minimum levels y_0^S and y_0^G of academic performance required for selection, y_0^S being required in category S and y_0^G in category G. These levels are not, however independent; they are linked by the condition which says that the total number selected must remain equal to N_0:

$$(y_1 - y_0^G)\alpha + (y_1 - h - y_0^G)(\beta - \beta_S) + (y_1 - h - y_0^S)\beta_S = N_0, \tag{6.17}$$

assuming that both y_0^G and y_0^S are smaller than $y_1 - h$. Obviously, it is still possible to impose the same requirement on everyone, that is to fix

$$y_0 = y_0^G = y_0^S. \tag{6.18}$$

---

[13] It is indeed a discrimination by segmentation that is permitted through this limited capacity of direct observation.

It is possible to abandon this uniform rule of selection. Is it desirable to do so?

This matter is at the heart of Allan Bakke's case. Mr Justice Brennan, Mr Justice White, Mr Justice Marshall, and Mr Justice Blackmun take the view that, 'When individual measurement is impossible or extremely impractical, there is nothing to prevent a State from using categorical means to achieve its ends, at least where the category is closely related to the goal.' Does our model support this view? To be able to give an answer, let us consider what happens if we fix

$$y_0^G > y_0 > y_0^S. \tag{6.19}$$

Then, if the differences $y_0^G - y_0$ and $y_0 - y_0^S$ are not too big, we find that we are led to select some individuals B belonging to category S who previously were not selected, and who have more ability than the individuals A who were previously selected and are now eliminated. We contribute in this way to the correction of both the inefficiency of the selection based on a uniform exigence y_0—in the sense that the average ability of the individuals selected increases— and that form of inequity that the uniform rule represents for the sub-population B. But category G is mixed. Enforcing (6.19) also has the effect of eliminating some individuals B belonging to category G who have greater ability than the newly selected individuals in category S. This effect contributes to a decrease in the average ability of those selected and creates a new form of inequity, this time between individuals B: those who are eliminated would be selected if they belonged to category S; they would also be selected if the uniform selection rule were re-established.

Clearly, there exists no rule of selection which, in the situations with incomplete information that we have here, can guarantee equity in any broadly acceptable sense. How do they compare from the point of view of efficiency? We can easily calculate that the average ability of the selected applicants is maximized when

$$y_0 - y_0^S = \frac{\alpha}{\alpha + \beta} h \tag{6.20}$$

or, equivalently, when

$$y_0^G - y_0^S = \frac{\alpha}{\alpha + \beta - \beta_S} h. \tag{6.21}$$

From (6.20), we can immediately conclude that it is efficient to have

$$y_0^S < y_0; \tag{6.22}$$

the selection rule should not be uniform. In other words, it is efficient to correct to some extent the imperfection of y as a signal of ω, despite the fact that the correction does not favour all of the individuals B.

From (6.21), we see that it is also efficient to have

$$y_0^G - y_0^S < h, \tag{6.23}$$

or

$$\omega_0^A < \omega_0^S, \tag{6.24}$$

knowing that ω_0^A is the minimum ability of a selected A while ω_0^S is the minimum ability of a selected B belonging to the category S. In other words, it is not efficient to correct the imperfection of y as a signal of ω to the point of assuring equal treatment on the basis of their abilities for individuals A and for individuals B of category S; the reason is that the correction does not extend to all individuals B.

This seems to support the aforementioned opinion expressed by Mr Justice Brennan, Mr Justice White, Mr Justice Marshall, and Mr Justice Blackmun, who also make clear that they see race or ethnic origin as a 'categorical means' that may legitimately be used in a selection process: 'Our prior cases unequivocally show that a State government may adopt race-conscious programs if the purpose of such programs is to remove the disparate racial impact its actions might otherwise have.'

When it comes to Allan Bakke's personal situation, the judgment reads as follows: 'Since petitioner [i.e. the University] could not satisfy its burden of proving that respondent [i.e. Allan Bakke] would not have been admitted even if there had been no special admissions program, he must be admitted.' While the decision itself might be warranted, the justification is not up to the mark; it is indeed in contradiction with (6.21), and it completely ignores the crucial question of whether Allan Bakke should be seen as a 'disadvantaged' applicant or not.[14]

3. Insurance and Solidarity

In this section we consider economic agents facing various risks and seeking insurance against these risks. There are also insurers ready to

---

[14] I.e. as an individual B in the category G, or as an individual A.

sell insurance contracts. However, as their information about who bears which risk is imperfect, they are unable to offer each subscriber the contract best suited to his particular situation. On the other hand, offering everybody the same contract might not be satisfactory. In between there is room for various discrimination devices (self-selection, segmentation, or a mix of both), the definition and appraisal of which is our objective in this section.

Let A be one of the agents seeking insurance. A faces a risk stemming from a random variable x taking the value x_1 $(0 < x_1)$ with probability $1 - \pi$, and the value x_2 $(0 < x_2 < x_1)$ with probability π, where $\pi < 1 - \pi$. For instance, x may be the income available to A; it is random in the sense that its value is dependent on a random event. If this event turns out to be favourable, x takes the value x_1, whereas if the event turns out to be unfavourable it takes the value x_2; an example of an unfavourable outcome would be an accident entailing a loss $L = x_1 - x_2$ with respect to the income x_1 available if the event turns out to be favourable, i.e. if no accident occurs. Agent A's random environment is entirely specified by the outcomes x_1 and x_2, and by the probabilities $1 - \pi$ and π which are attached to them, with π appearing in our example as the probability of an accident causing the loss L.

The population we will consider in this section is made up of two types of such agents, say A' and A''. Both face a risk stemming from a random variable x^0, with outcomes x_1^0 and x_2^0 $(0 < x_2^0 < x_1^0)$, and both have the same von Neumann–Morgenstern function v.[15] But the probabilities differ: the random variable x^0 takes the value x_2^0 with probability π' in the case of A', and with probability π'' in the case of A'', with $\pi' < \pi''$. Then the two types differ only in that A'' is exposed to a greater risk of suffering the loss $L = x_1^0 - x_2^0$. This sole difference is still sufficient for A' and A'' to have different utility functions. For A', in fact,

$$U'(X) = E'\{v(x)\} = (1 - \pi')v(x_1) + \pi'v(x_2) \qquad (6.25)$$

while for A'',

$$U''(X) = E''\{v(x)\} = (1 - \pi'')v(x_1) + \pi''v(x_2). \qquad (6.26)$$

Comparing (6.25) and (6.26), we have

$$E'\{v(x^0)\} - E''\{v(x^0)\} = (\pi'' - \pi')\{v(x_1^0) - v(x_2^0)\} > 0.$$

---

[15] On some basic concepts of consumer choice in the presence of risk, see Sec. A3 of the Appendix.

Combined with (A36) of the Appendix, this implies that $\alpha' < \alpha''$: as he is exposed to a greater risk—in the sense that the probability of the unfavourable event is greater—A" is ready to pay more than A' for the reduction of the difference between x_1^0 and x_2^0.

Imagine a population composed in proportions v' and v'' ($v' + v'' = 1$) of agents A' and A", or in other words of risks of the first and second types.[16] If the total population is N, the population for each of the two types is $N' = v'N$ and $N'' = v''N$, respectively. If, in each type, the risks are sufficiently numerous and stochastically well adapted, then an insurer who would be capable, without error or cost, of assigning each agent to his type could offer to each agent A' a contract with a premium equal to $\alpha_n' = \pi'L$ and the indemnity L, and to each agent A" a contract with a higher premium, equal to $\alpha_n'' = \pi''L$, and the same indemnity L. Doing this, the insurer balances his revenue and his average outlay. But such an identification may be impossible or too costly to realize. When a risk solicits a contract, the insurer would then be incapable of assigning him to a type, even if he knows, as is usually the case, the proportions v' and v'', perhaps from a representative sample.

Under these conditions, one possible policy for the insurer is to offer the same contract to each of the N risks, i.e. to treat them uniformly despite the difference in types. The only contract providing all insured full coverage while balancing the insurer's budget embodies the premium $\bar{\alpha}_n = \bar{\pi}L$ and the indemnity L, where

$$\bar{\pi} = v'\pi' + v''\pi''. \qquad (6.27)$$

This contract is represented in Figure 6.6 by the point $\bar{X}$ such that the ratio of its distances from the points M' and M'' is $(\bar{\pi} - \pi')/(\pi'' - \bar{\pi})$. The revenue $N\bar{\pi}L$ equals the average outlay $N'\pi'L + N''\pi''L$. However, each risk A' pays more than the premium α_n' which would suffice for budget balance within this type of risk, when it is isolated from the other one; the excess payment over α_n' is

$$\bar{\tau} = \bar{\alpha}_n - \alpha_n' = (\bar{\pi} - \pi')L. \qquad (6.28)$$

Meanwhile, each risk A" benefits from a subsidy

$$\bar{\sigma} = \alpha_n'' - \bar{\alpha}_n = (\pi'' - \bar{\pi})L. \qquad (6.29)$$

In other words, for each contract $(\bar{\alpha}_n, L)$ purchased by a risk A', the insurer makes a profit $\bar{\tau}$, and for each contract $(\bar{\alpha}_n, L)$ purchased by a risk A", he carries a loss $\bar{\sigma}$.

---

[16] It is convenient to identify an agent with the risk to which he is exposed.

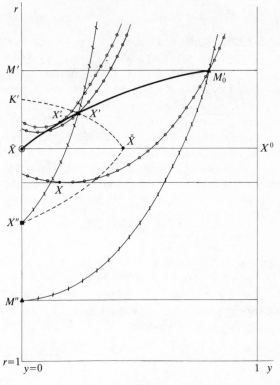

Fig. 6.6

The insurer will also balance revenue and outlay if, instead of signing a contract $(\bar{\alpha}_n, L)$ providing full coverage, he signs with each of the N agents a contract $\{(1 - \bar{y})\bar{\alpha}_n, (1 - \bar{y})L\}$ providing only partial coverage. Such a contract is represented in Figure 6.6 by any point $\bar{\bar{X}}$ on the segment $X^0 \bar{X}$.[17] Contract $\bar{\bar{X}}$ leads, for each risk A', to the excess payment

$$\bar{\bar{\tau}} = (1 - \bar{y})\bar{\tau}, \tag{6.30}$$

and, for each risk A'', to the subsidy

$$\bar{\bar{\sigma}} = (1 - \bar{y})\bar{\sigma}. \tag{6.31}$$

For the insurer, $\bar{\bar{\tau}}$ is a profit and $\bar{\bar{\sigma}}$ is a loss. For budget balance, we

[17] The equation of the straight line supporting $X^0 \bar{X}$ is $r = 1/\bar{\pi}$.

must have

$$N'\bar{\tau} = N''\bar{\sigma} \qquad (6.32)$$

which is immediately derived from (6.27), (6.30), and (6.31).

Any contract on the arc $\bar{X}K'$, when purchased by a risk A', brings the insurer the same profit $\bar{\tau}$. Similarly, any contract on the arc $\bar{X}X''$, when purchased by a risk A'', brings the same loss $\bar{\sigma}$. Consequently, the balance of revenue and outlay is still realized when the N' risks A' each subscribe to a contract on $\bar{X}K'$ and, simultaneously, the N'' risks A'' each subscribe to a contract on $\bar{X}X''$. To actually obtain this distribution of subscriptions, it is necessary that the contract offered on $\bar{X}X''$ be no less attractive for a risk A'' than the contract simultaneously offered on $\bar{X}K'$. This condition is fulfilled by the pair X', X'', where X' on $\bar{X}K'$ is indifferent to X'' for a risk A'':

$$U''(X') = U''(X'').$$

We have indeed a stronger property: of all the contracts on $\bar{X}X''$, X'' is preferred by A'', while of all the contracts on $\bar{X}X'$, X' is preferred by A'. In other words, indicating by $\tau(\Xi')$ the excess payment from a risk A' who subscribes to the contract Ξ', and by $\sigma(\Xi'')$ the subsidy to a risk A'' who subscribes to the contract Ξ'', it appears that the pair of contracts X', X'' is the solution of the problem

$$\max_{\Xi',\,\Xi''} U'(\Xi') \qquad (6.33)$$

$$\text{s.t.} \quad U''(\Xi') \leqslant U''(\Xi'')$$
$$\sigma(\Xi'') = \bar{\sigma}$$
$$N'\tau(\Xi') = N''\sigma(\Xi'')$$

where $\bar{\sigma}$ is a fixed parameter. The first of these constraints is a condition of incentive compatibility: contracts Ξ' and Ξ'' must be such that each risk A'' chooses Ξ'' rather than Ξ'. This condition is least constraining for $\Xi'' = X''$. From the second constraint, Ξ'' must also be such that a risk A'' benefits from a subsidy equal to $\bar{\sigma}$ when he subscribes to Ξ''. The third condition, which may also be written

$$\tau(\Xi') = \bar{\tau},$$

is the budget balance condition for the insurer.

With the level of subsidy fixed at $\bar{\sigma}$, the best offer for both types of risks is thus the pair of contracts X', X''. The discrimination between types operates through self-selection: the excess payment implied by the contract X' to which a risk A' subscribes is just high enough to deter a risk A'' from subscribing to this contract rather than to contract X''.

Contracts X' and X'', which constitute the solution to the problem (6.33), are functions $X'(\bar{\sigma})$ and $X''(\bar{\sigma})$ of the parameter $\bar{\sigma}$; $\bar{X}$ is of course also a function $\bar{X}(\bar{\sigma})$ of $\bar{\sigma}$. For $\bar{\sigma} = 0$, we have (see Figures 6.6 or 6.7)

$$\bar{X}(0) = X^0$$
$$X'(0) = M'_0$$
$$X''(0) = M''.$$

As there is no subsidy in this case, $\bar{\tau} = 0$ and budget balance is realized within each type of risks. On the other hand, for $\bar{\sigma} = \bar{\sigma}$, we have

$$\bar{X}(\bar{\sigma}) = X'(\bar{\sigma}) = X''(\bar{\sigma}) = \bar{X};$$

all the risks subscribe to the same contract.

When $\bar{\sigma}$ grows from 0 to $\bar{\sigma}$, it is clear that U'' increases from $v(x_1^0 - \alpha_n'')$ to $v(x_1^0 - \alpha_n'' + \bar{\sigma})$, whereas the profile of U' depends on v'. Indeed, when v' is large ($\bar{X}$ is relatively close to M') the excess payment τ for a given $\bar{\sigma}$ is relatively small:

$$\bar{\tau} = \frac{(1 - v')\bar{\sigma}}{v'}.$$

It is then possible that the inconvenience for each risk A' resulting from an increase in $\bar{\sigma}$ is more than compensated for by the advantage that A' derives from the alleviation of the incentive compatibility constraint $U''\{X'(\bar{\sigma})\} \leqslant U''\{X''(\bar{\sigma})\}$.

Two different cases emerge:

1. v' is sufficiently large so that $U'\{X'(0)\}$ does not maximize $U'\{X'(\bar{\sigma})\}$ on $[0, \bar{\sigma}]$. Then let $\bar{\sigma}_*$ be a value of $\bar{\sigma}$ which maximizes U' on $[0, \bar{\sigma}]$, and let (see Figure 6.6)

$$X'_* = X'(\bar{\sigma}_*)$$
$$X''_* = X''(\bar{\sigma}_*)$$

be the corresponding contracts to which A' and A'' respectively subscribe.

2. $U'\{X'(\bar{\sigma})\}$ reaches its maximum on $[0, \bar{\sigma}]$ at $\bar{\sigma} = 0$. In other words, $\bar{\sigma}_* = 0$ and (see Figure 6.7)

$$X'_* = X'(0) = M'_0$$
$$X''_* = X''(0) = M''$$

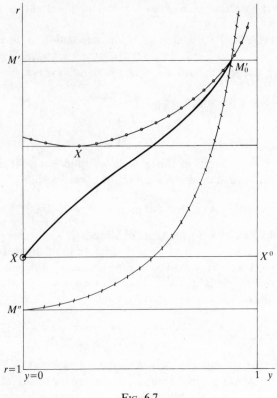

FIG. 6.7

By eliminating the parameter $\bar{\sigma}$ between

$$U' = U'\{X'(\bar{\sigma})\}$$

and

$$U'' = U''\{X''(\bar{\sigma})\},$$

we obtain U' as a function of U'', as depicted in Figures 6.8 (corresponding to case 1) and 6.9 (corresponding to case 2). In both cases, the arc $a'a''$ represents the set of second-best Pareto optima, subject to the existing constraints: the insurer's budget balance constraint, and the incentive compatibility constraint. Now, among those optima, which is to be chosen? There is of course no purely economic answer to this question, which is fundamentally of a distributive nature. If we are dealing with risks affecting people's

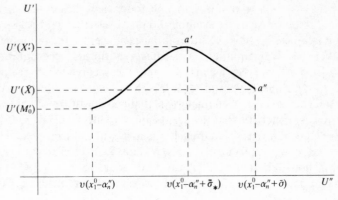

FIG. 6.8

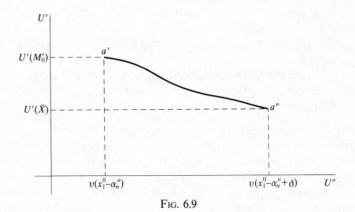

FIG. 6.9

health, and the insurance corrects in part the effects of handicaps, it might be considered socially desirable to alleviate the effects of these handicaps as much as possible; all the concerned agents would then be offered the sole contract $\bar{X}$. This is the spirit of the approach taken by the British national health service and by the French social security. On the other hand, for other kinds of risks which are less a matter for solidarity, it might seem reasonable not to ask the 'good' risks to subsidize the 'bad' ones beyond the level $\bar{\sigma}_*$ (corresponding to a' on Figures 6.8 and 6.9), that best suits their own interests.

Let us assume now that it is possible to segment the population of risks; our objective is to examine how self-selection and segmentation interact and how the situation of each agent is then modified. Let there be a segmentation in two categories, the first incorporating N_1' agents A' and N_1'' agents A'', and the second incorporating $N_2' = N' - N_1'$ agents A' and $N_2'' = N'' - N_1''$ agents A''. Membership in a category is due to a characteristic that is costlessly observable; it is also a characteristic that the agent cannot easily change.[18] On the other hand, the risk type of each agent is still indiscernable. The ratios $\mu_1 = N_1'/N_1''$ and $\mu_2 = N_2'/N_2''$ inside each category are known, however. If μ_1 and μ_2 are both equal to $\mu = N'/N''$, the segmentation has no effect; so let us assume, for instance, that $\mu_1 > \mu_2$.

To be able to appraise the effects of the segmentation, we need to use the particular value of μ, say $\tilde{\mu}$, such that

— for $\mu > \tilde{\mu}$, an optimal offer from the point of view of the risks A' is a pair of contracts X_*', X_*'', which is different from the pair M_0', M''; this corresponds to the case represented in Figures 6.6 and 6.8;

— for $\mu < \tilde{\mu}$, the optimal offer from the point of view of the risks A' is the pair M_0', M''; this corresponds to the case represented in Figures 6.7 and 6.9.

If $\mu > \tilde{\mu}$, then the members of the first category all benefit from the segmentation, while the members of the second category all suffer, for the burden on the A' of financing the subsidies to the A'' becomes lighter in the first category and heavier in the second. If $\mu < \tilde{\mu}$, then no one will suffer from the segmentation. If, furthermore, $\mu_1 > \tilde{\mu}$, then members of the first category will actually benefit: compared with the number N_1'' of risks A'' belonging to the first category, the number N_1' of risks A' of the same category is sufficiently large that they benefit from subsidizing the A''. The segmentation then distinguishes a subset of agents for whom a threshold is reached, a threshold from which financial arrangements between types permit a lesser signalling effort.

---

[18] One of the largest insurers in France is the Mutuelle Assurance des Instituteurs de France. Membership is restricted to teachers and their families; the proportion of 'good' risks is significantly higher than in the general population, and the contracts offered far more attractive. This case has counterparts in other European countries, and in other professions.

The segmentation however can benefit all of the agents, even for $\mu > \tilde{\mu}$, if it is accompanied by a tax on the agents who benefit directly from it, in this case the members of the first category (as $\mu_1 > \mu_2$). To see this, while avoiding heavy calculations, consider a segmentation for which $N''_1 = 0$. The first category then is made up solely of agents A', who benefit directly from the situation since they are offered a contract M'. On the other hand the members of the second category, whether they are A' or A'', must put up with contracts less advantageous than X'_* and X''_*, which are the contracts they buy before the segmentation takes place.

However, it is possible to tax the N'_1 agents of the first category by demanding from each of them, on top of the premium $\pi'L$ embodied in the contract M', a tax t. In order that the tax does not decrease their utility to a level less than $U'(X'_*)$, t cannot be larger than t_{max} such that

$$v(x_1^0 - \pi'L - t_{max}) = U(X'_*).$$

The revenue from this tax is then at most $N'_1 t_{max}$. Would this suffice to make good the deficit left to the agents of the second category by the departure of N'_1 agents A'? Before this departure, the sum of the excess payments from the risks A', equal to the subsidies to the risks A'', was $N'\tau(X'_*)$, with

$$\tau(X'_*) = \{(1 - \pi')x_1^0 + \pi'x_2^0\} - \{(1 - \pi')x'_{*1} + \pi'x'_{*2}\}.$$

The departure of N'_1 agents A' leaves the deficit $N'_1\tau(X'_*)$. Is this inferior to $N'_1 t_{max}$? In other words, do we have

$$v\{x_1^0 - \pi'L - \tau(x'_x)\} > U'(X'_*)?$$

or, still again,

$$v\{(1 - \pi')x'_{*1} + \pi'x'_{*2}\} > (1 - \pi')v(x'_{*1}) + \pi'v(x'_{*2})?$$

Since v is strictly concave, the answer is affirmative. Therefore a well adjusted tax can distribute the benefits in such a manner that everybody finds himself in a situation more advantageous than before segmentation is introduced. This result holds even when the segmentation is not as simple as that we have just considered here (assuming $N''_1 = 0$).

Appendix

A.1. Some Basic Notions of Microeconomics in a Simple Framework

Techniques and production functions

In this section we consider an economy which comprises only two persons (call them A and B), who are isolated from the rest of the world for a certain period of time. In order to support themselves during that period, they have available initial resources and a technique of production. The initial resources consist of y_0 units of a good (call it Y), which they can either consume directly or transform into another good (call it X), which they can also use for consumption but not for production. The transformation is realized with the technique of production they have available. In this simple economy there are only two consumers, two goods, and one technique of production; in a less simple one, there would be any number of consumers, any number of goods, and any number of techniques, but the results presented below would still hold.

The technique of production makes it possible to get at most $f(y_x)$ units of good X from y_x units of good Y; in other words, $f(y_x)$ is the maximum output obtainable from the input y_x with the technique at hand. The function f is called a production function; we assume that it is increasing in y_x unless it is equal to zero (for a few examples, see Figure A1). Its derivative $f' = \mathrm{d}f/\mathrm{d}y_x$, provided it exists, is called the marginal rate of transformation of Y into X; $\mathrm{d}x = f'\mathrm{d}y_x$ is indeed the extra output that can be obtained from the extra input $\mathrm{d}y_x$. Conversely, $(1/f')\mathrm{d}x$ is the input that can be saved by reducing the output by $\mathrm{d}x$; $1/f'$ is the marginal rate of transformation of X into Y.

In Figure A1, four examples of production functions are depicted. The production function in part (a) is linear, of the form $f(y_x) = ay_x$, with $a > 0$. It corresponds to a technique that exhibits constant returns to scale, i.e. a technique such that multiplying the input by any positive number multiplies the output by the same number.

The production function in part (b) is concave: if y_x' and y_x'' are any

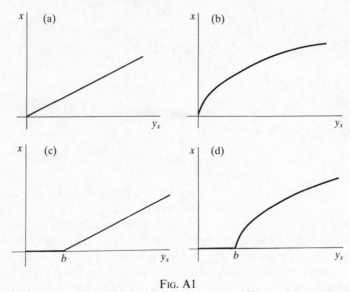

Fig. A1

two non-negative numbers, any convex combination $\delta y_x' + (1 - \delta)y_x''$ of these numbers, with $0 < \delta < 1$, is such that

$$f\{\delta y_x' + (1 - \delta)y_x''\} > \delta f(y_x') + (1 - \delta)f(y_x'').$$

For example, $f(y_x) = a(y_x)^\alpha$, with $a > 0$ and $0 < \alpha < 1$, is concave. A concave production function corresponds to a technique that exhibits decreasing returns to scale, i.e. a technique such that, for any input y_x and any real number k greater than 1, the output from ky_x is less than k times the output from y_x:

$$f(ky_x) < kf(y_x) \qquad \text{for any } k > 1.$$

The production functions in parts (c) and (d) differ from those in parts (a) and (b) respectively, only in that they exhibit a fixed cost: producing any output, however small, requires the prior disposal of an amount b of good Y. For example, instead of $f(y_x) = a(y_x)^\alpha$, the production function in part (d) reads:

$$f(y_x) = 0 \qquad \text{if } 0 \leqslant y_x \leqslant b$$
$$f(y_x) = a(y_x - b)^\alpha \qquad \text{if } b \leqslant y_x.$$

The four production functions represented in Figure A1 do satisfy the assumption that we have introduced above: they are increasing unless they are equal to zero.

Consumers' preferences and utility functions

In order to make the link between production decisions and consumers' preferences, we shall now indicate how such preferences are described in microeconomics. Take person A, for example. He might think of consuming x'_A units of good X and y'_A units of good Y, with $x'_A \geqslant 0$ and $y'_A \geqslant 0$; i.e., he might think of consuming a consumption bundle, as it is called, composed of x'_A units of X and y'_A units of Y.[1] A might also think of consuming x''_A units of X and y''_A units of Y, with $x''_A \geqslant 0$ and $y''_A \geqslant 0$. We assume that, given any two bundles (x'_A, y'_A) and (x''_A, y''_A), A knows whether he prefers (x'_A, y'_A), or whether he prefers (x''_A, y''_A), or whether he is indifferent between the two. We also assume that A prefers to have more of a good rather than less, i.e. that he prefers (x'_A, y'_A) to (x''_A, y''_A) as soon as $x'_A \geqslant x''_A$ and $y'_A \geqslant y''_A$, with at least one strict inequality. Finally, we assume that A's preferences can be represented by a utility function and that this function is bounded and continuous.

More precisely, this last assumption reads: there exists a function U_A, bounded and continuous, which associates a real number $U_A(x_A, y_A)$ to every bundle (x_A, y_A) is such way that

$$U_A(x'_A, y'_A) > U_A(x''_A, y''_A) \qquad \text{if A prefers } (x'_A, y'_A);$$

$$U_A(x'_A, y'_A) < U_A(x''_A, y''_A) \qquad \text{if A prefers } (x''_A, y''_A);$$

$$U_A(x'_A, y'_A) = U_A(x''_A, y''_A) \qquad \text{if A is indifferent between the two.}$$

From what we have assumed on the preferences, U_A is obviously increasing in both x_A and y_A. It is worth stressing that we do not assume that A is consciously using a utility function to rank the consumption bundles; things just happen as if he were.[2] Since U_A is bounded and has a purely ordinal meaning, there is no restriction to assume that it is non-negative; from now on, we will take that for granted.

---

[1] This bundle can be identified with the point (x'_A, y'_A) in a plane. More generally, a consumption bundle can be identified with a point in a Euclidean space the dimension of which is equal to the number of goods for consumption in the economy.

[2] A preference preordering which is complete and continuous can indeed be represented by some utility function; for a rigorous statement and a proof, see Debreu (1954). Preference preorderings and utility functions are discussed at length in Malinvaud (1985) and in Varian (1984); Varian (1987) is written at a lower level of generality and is easier to read. It should be noticed that U_A has a purely ordinal meaning, hence is defined up to an increasing transformation: if g is an increasing real-valued function defined on the real numbers, $g \circ U_A$ is a utility function representing the same preferences as U_A does.

The utility function U_A can be visualized by a set of indifference curves, each of which is the subset of all the bundles indifferent to any of them, that is of all the bundles giving U_A some common value; when there are more than two goods for consumption in the economy, one speaks of 'indifference surfaces'. In Figure A2, for example, the curve Γ_1 is the subset of all the bundles that are indifferent to (x'_A, y'_A), i.e. of all the bundles giving U_A the value $U_A(x'_A, y'_A)$. The same relationship holds between Γ_2 and $U_A\{\alpha x'_A + (1-\alpha)x''_A, \alpha y'_A + (1-\alpha)y''_A\}$, as between Γ_3 and $U_A(x''_A, y''_A)$, with

$$U_A(x'_A, y'_A) < U_A\{\alpha x'_A + (1-\alpha)x''_A,$$
$$\alpha y'_A + (1-\alpha)y''_A\} < U_A(x''_A, y''_A).$$

We thus see that representing A's preferences by a utility function amounts to labelling A's indifference curves with real numbers.

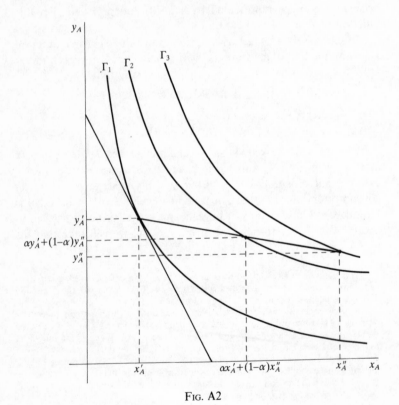

FIG. A2

The indifference curves depicted in Figure A2 correspond to a quasi-concave utility function.[3] A quasi-concave utility function expresses a liking for diversity in consumption rather than specialization.

The quotient of the partial derivatives of U_A, provided they exist,

$$\pi_A(x_A, y_A) = \frac{\partial U_A / \partial x_A}{\partial U_A / \partial y_A},$$

is called A's marginal rate of substitution of good Y for good X; A is indeed indifferent between the bundle (x_A, y_A) and the bundle obtained from (x_A, y_A) by adding (resp. subtracting) dx_A to x_A and subtracting (resp. adding) $dy_A = \pi_A(x_A, y_A)dx_A$ from y_A.[4] When U_A is quasi-concave, then, along any indifference curve, the marginal rate of substitution $\pi_A(x_A, y_A)$ is decreasing with x_A increasing, or equivalently with y_A decreasing: an additional amount of X becomes less valuable in terms of Y as the available amount of X relative to the available amount of Y increases.

Feasible allocations and Pareto-efficient allocations

The initial resources of the economy and its production function set the limits to the simultaneous availability of goods X and Y for consumption: if the quantity y_x of Y, with $0 \leqslant y_x \leqslant y_0$, is used as an input in the production of X, then $f(y_x)$ and $y_0 - y_x$ are the maximum quantities of goods X and Y available for consumption. In other words, the non-negative quantities of goods X and Y consumed respectively by A and B—we denote them by x_A, y_A, x_B, and y_B, and we say that they constitute an allocation (x_A, y_A, x_B, y_B)—

---

[3] There are two equivalent ways of defining quasi-concavity:

(a) U_A is quasi-concave if and only if, for any bundle (x_A, y_A), the set of all bundles preferred or indifferent to (x_A, y_A) is convex.

(b) U_A is quasi-concave if and only if, for any two bundles (x'_A, y'_A) and (x''_A, y''_A), any convex combination $(\delta x'_A + (1-\delta)x''_A, \ \delta y'_A + (1-\delta)y''_A)$ of these bundles, with $0 < \delta < 1$, is preferred to the least preferred of them.

[4] A is indifferent between (x_A, y_A), $\{x_A + dx_A, y_A - \pi_A(x_A, y_A)dx_A\}$ and $\{x_A - dx_A, y_A + \pi_A(x_A, y_A)dx_A\}$; e.g.

$$U_A\{x_A - dx_A, y_A + \pi_A(x_A, y_A)dx_A\} = U_A(x_A, y_A) - \frac{\partial U_A}{\partial x_A}dx_A + \frac{\partial U_A}{\partial y_A}\pi_A(x_A, y_A)dx_A$$

$$= U_A(x_A, y_A).$$

must satisfy the economy's scarcity constraints:[5]

$$y_A + y_B + y_x \leqslant y_0 \qquad (A1)$$

$$x_A + x_B \leqslant f(y_x) \qquad (A2)$$

for some y_x with $0 \leqslant y_x \leqslant y_0$. The allocations (x_A, y_A, x_B, y_B) that satisfy these constraints are called the 'feasible allocations' of the economy; let $\mathscr{F}$ denote the set of all such allocations.

Among the feasible allocations of the economy, some are inefficient in the following sense: the feasible allocation (x'_A, y'_A, x'_B, y'_B) is inefficient if there exists a feasible allocation $(x''_A, y''_A, x''_B, y''_B)$ that one consumer prefers to (x'_A, y'_A, x'_B, y'_B), the other consumer having the same preference or being just indifferent between the two allocations;[6] one says that the allocation $(x''_A, y''_A, x''_B, y''_B)$ Pareto-dominates the allocation (x'_A, y'_A, x'_B, y'_B). When there is no such allocation $(x''_A, y''_A, x''_B, y''_B)$, then (x'_A, y'_A, x'_B, y'_B) is called a Pareto-efficient or Pareto-optimal allocation, also a Pareto optimum.[7] Thus an allocation is Pareto-efficient if and only if there exists no feasible change of this allocation which would make a consumer better off without making the other consumer[8] worse off. Let $\mathscr{E}$ denote the set of all Pareto-efficient allocations; $\mathscr{E}$ is of course a subset of the set $\mathscr{F}$ of all feasible allocations.

Consider any feasible allocation, say (x'_A, y'_A, x'_B, y'_B), and denote by u_B the value $U_B(x'_B, y'_B)$ that B's utility takes at the bundle (x'_B, y'_B). An alternative way of defining Pareto efficiency is then: (x'_A, y'_A, x'_B, y'_B) is Pareto-efficient if and only if it maximizes U_A among all feasible allocations (x_A, y_A, x_B, y_B) which are such that $U_B(x_B, y_B) \geqslant u_B$. By varying u_B between the minimum and maximum values

---

[5] In this very simple economy, there are only two goods; hence there are only two scarcity constraints.

[6] For instance, A prefers $(x''_A, y''_A, x''_B, y''_B)$, meaning that he prefers the bundle (x''_A, y''_A) that this allocation grants him to the bundle (x'_A, y'_A) that the allocation (x'_A, y'_A, x'_B, y'_B) grants him. Simultaneously, B prefers (x''_B, y''_B) to (x'_B, y'_B) or is indifferent between the two.

[7] Named after Vilfredo Pareto, who introduced the concept in his *Manuel d' Economie Politique* (1906). The words 'optimal' and 'optimum' have become set through common use but might be misunderstood: there is here no idea of absolute dominance, since a particular Pareto-efficient allocation usually dominates, in the sense defined above, only *some* inefficient allocations, and not all of them. Usually, there is also a large number of Pareto-efficient allocations. On balance, every inefficient allocation is dominated by at least one Pareto-efficient one. The notion of Pareto dominance has thus a limited range; and, conversely, the requirement of efficiency on which it rests is minimal.

[8] In an economy with more than two consumers, we would say instead: without making *any other consumer* worse off.

that U_B takes over $\mathscr{F}$, we obtain in this way all the Pareto-efficient allocations of the economy, wich make up the subset $\mathscr{E}$ of $\mathscr{F}$.

To every feasible allocation (x_A, y_A, x_B, y_B), there is associated a utility distribution $U_A(x_A, y_A)$, $U_B(x_B, y_B)$, which can be represented by a point in the plane with coordinates U_A, U_B. The image $\Psi(\mathscr{F})$ of $\mathscr{F}$ by this function, which we denote by Ψ, is called the 'utility possibility set'; it is a bounded subset of the positive orthant in the plane U_A, U_B (see Figure A3). The image $\Psi(\mathscr{E})$ of $\mathscr{E}$ by Ψ is called the 'utility possibility frontier'; it bounds the utility possibility set. From the definition of Pareto-efficient allocations, it is clear that $\Psi(\mathscr{E})$ has a negative slope. Any point inside the frontier $\Psi(\mathscr{E})$ corresponds to an allocation that is inefficient. On the other hand, any point outside the frontier is not feasible, i.e. is inaccessible given the available initial resources and technique. Finally, moving along the frontier would improve the lot of one consumer to the detriment of the other.

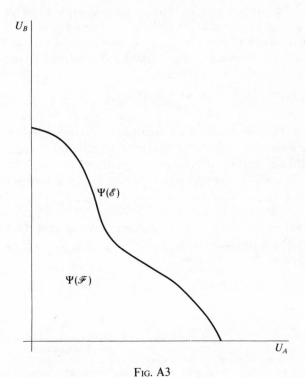

Fig. A3

The allocations that maximize U_A among all feasible allocations such that U_B is greater than or equal to some predetermined level u_B are the solutions of the constrained maximization problem:[9]

$$\max U_A(x_A, y_A) \tag{A3}$$
$$\text{s.t.} \quad U_B(x_B, y_B) - u_B = 0 \qquad (\mu)$$
$$f(y_x) - x_A - x_B = 0 \qquad (p)$$
$$y_0 - y_A - y_B - y_x = 0 \qquad (q)$$

Moreover the five variables in this problem, i.e. x_A, y_A, x_B, y_B, and y_x, cannot be negative. We could have eliminated y_x by contracting the last two constraints into one, but we prefer to keep them separate as they are economically significant, being the scarcity constraints on the two goods available in the economy; in particular, we want to exhibit the economic interpretation of the Lagrange multipliers p and q that we will associate with them.

To each constraint we indeed associate a real number, which is called a Lagrange multiplier, and which will work as an auxiliary variable. The Lagrange multipliers (here: μ, p, and q) are also called the 'dual variables', whereas the pre-existing variables (here: x_A, y_A, x_B, y_B, y_x) are called the 'primal variables'. The following function of both primal and dual variables,

$$\mathscr{L}(x_A, y_A, x_B, y_B, y_x; \mu, p, q) = U_A(x_A, y_A) + \lambda U_B(x_B, y_B) + p\{f(y_x) - x_A - x_B\} + q(y_0 - y_A - y_B - y_x),$$

is called the Lagrangean of the constrained maximization problem. Its usefulness stems from the general mathematical property that, provided it is differentiable, necessary conditions for the problem are easily obtained by deriving it with respect to the primal variables. More precisely, a set of positive[10] values x_A^*, y_A^*, x_B^*, y_B^*, y_x^*, for the primal variables is a solution of the problem only if there exists some set of values μ^*, p^*, q^*, for the dual variables so that the following conditions are satisfied at $x_A = x_A^*$, $y_A = y_A^*$, $x_B = x_B^*$, $y_B = y_B^*$, $y_x = y_x^*$, $\mu = \mu^*$, $p = p^*$, $q = q^*$:

$$\frac{\partial \mathscr{L}}{\partial x_A} = 0$$

---

[9] Because f, U_A, and U_B are increasing, writing the constraints under the form of equalities is equivalent to writing them under the form of inequalities.

[10] When some of them are not positive, i.e. are zero, then the non-negativity constraints are binding and the necessary conditions are somewhat more complicated.

$$\frac{\partial \mathscr{L}}{\partial y_A} = 0$$

$$\frac{\partial \mathscr{L}}{\partial x_B} = 0$$

$$\frac{\partial \mathscr{L}}{\partial y_B} = 0$$

$$\frac{\partial \mathscr{L}}{\partial y_x} = 0.$$

These conditions are called the 'first-order necessary conditions' for the constrained maximization problem: at a solution, the first-order derivative of the Lagrangean with respect to each primal variable is equal to zero. In the economy considered here, these conditions take the form

$$\frac{\partial U_A}{\partial x_A} - p = 0 \tag{A4}$$

$$\frac{\partial U_A}{\partial y_A} - q = 0 \tag{A5}$$

$$\mu \frac{\partial U_B}{\partial x_B} - p = 0 \tag{A6}$$

$$\mu \frac{\partial U_B}{\partial y_B} - q = 0 \tag{A7}$$

$$-q + pf' = 0. \tag{A8}$$

Eliminating μ, p, and q, one gets the conditions

$$\pi_A(x_A, y_A) = \pi_B(x_B, y_B) = \frac{1}{f'}, \tag{A9}$$

which mean that, at a Pareto-efficient allocation, A and B have the same marginal rate of substitution of Y for X, and that this common rate of substitution is equal to the marginal rate of transformation of X into Y. They are all equal to the ratio of the corresponding Lagrange multipliers p and q. In the next section we will interpret p and q as the prices of goods X and Y, respectively.

One easily understands why conditions (A9) must be satisfied at a Pareto-efficient allocation. Indeed, suppose that they are not, for example suppose that $\pi_A(x_A, y_A) > 1/f'$. Then, loosely speaking, it is possible to increase A's utility by simultaneously giving him one extra unit of X and taking from him $1/f'$ units of Y. This switch is itself made possible by putting $1/f'$ extra units of Y into the production of X, hence producing one extra unit of X. A being better off and B not affected, (x_A, y_A, x_B, y_B) cannot be Pareto-efficient.

Efficiency and prices

In this subsection we will see how it is possible, when certain conditions are met,[11] to interpret the Lagrange multipliers p^* and q^* (associated with the scarcity constraints) as prices, and to use them in order to implement the Pareto-efficient allocation $(x_A^*, y_A^*, x_B^*, y_B^*)$. We will first consider the production side, then the consumption side.

The firm: taking prices and maximizing profit. Assume that the responsibility for producing X from Y with technique f is given to a firm and that this firm adopts the following line of conduct: among all feasible production plans (x, y_x), that is all plans that satisfy $x \leqslant f(y_x)$, the firm realizes one that maximizes $p^* x - q^* y_x$. In other words, the firm is told that p^* is the price at which it may sell its output and q^* the price at which it may buy its input; on this basis, it maximizes its profit $p^* x - q^* y_x$.

For the firm, p^* and q^* are fixed parameters which it takes as given, whereas x and y_x are decision variables. A firm behaving in this manner is called a price-taking firm or a competitive firm: it makes no attempt to modify the prices that it faces. When there is just one firm, as is the case in the simple economy considered here, some form of intervention would seem necessary to have the firm behave as a price-taking firm. Without such intervention, the firm would rather behave as a monopoly which tries to manipulate prices.[12] When there is a large number of firms—none of them being significantly bigger than the others—selling the same good on the same market, there is no incentive for any of them, individually, to try and influence the competitive process from which the price of the good results. They are all price-taking firms, also called 'competitive firms' with reference to the competitive process in which they are involved.

---

[11] These are conditions on the production and the utility functions, as well as conditions on the behaviours of the economic agents; we will be more precise later in this section.

[12] As in ch. 5.

As f is an increasing function, the feasible production plans that maximize the firm's profit at prices p^* and q^* are the solutions of the constrained maximization problem

$$\max p^* x - q^* y_x$$
$$\text{s.t. } f(y_x) - x = 0. \qquad (A10)$$

A geometric approach immediately suggests[13] (see Figure A4(a))

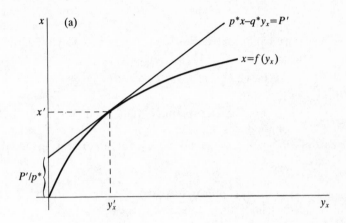

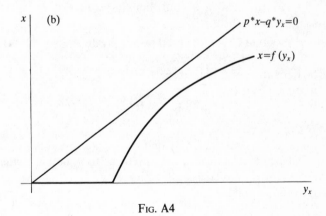

Fig. A4

[13] Provided f is differentiable and both x' and y_x' are positive; see Figure A4(b) for a case where $(x', y_x') = (0, 0)$.

that, at a solution (x', y'_x) of this problem, the isoprofit line

$$p^*x - q^*y_x = P'$$

is tangent to the curve

$$x = f(y_x)$$

representing the technical constraint; P' is the profit $p^*x' - q^*y'_x$ obtained from the production plan (x', y'_x). In other words, at (x', y'_x), one has

$$p^* = q^* \frac{1}{f'}. \tag{A11}$$

This necessary condition is obtained in a rigorous way by deriving the Lagrangean

$$\mathscr{L}(x, y_x; \lambda) = p^*x - q^*y_x + \lambda\{f(y_x) - x\}$$

with respect to x and y_x.

In order to produce the quantity x of good X, the quantity $y_x = f^{-1}(x)$ of good Y is required as input. The price of Y being q^*, the cost of producing x is therefore q^*y_x. It is an increasing function of x, namely

$$C(x) = q^*f^{-1}(x). \tag{A12}$$

If f is linear (constant returns to scale), C is linear as well. If f is concave (decreasing returns to scale), C is convex.[14]

If there is a fixed cost C_0, then C has a discontinuity at $x = 0$:[15]

$$C(0) = 0 \quad \text{but} \quad \lim_{\substack{x \to 0 \\ x > 0}} C(x) = C_0;$$

and one says that $C(x)$ is the total cost of producing x, C_0 is the fixed cost, and $C(x) - C_0$ is the variable cost.

The derivative of C with respect to x, provided it exists, is called the marginal cost c:

$$c(x) = \frac{dC}{dx}.$$

Constant returns to scale imply that the marginal cost is a constant, i.e. is independent of x; decreasing returns to scale imply that the marginal cost is an increasing function of x.

From (A12), one has

$$c(x) = q^* \frac{1}{f'}, \tag{A13}$$

[14] See Figure A5(a) and (b), which, respectively, correspond to figure A1(a) and (b).
[15] See Figure A5(c) and (d).

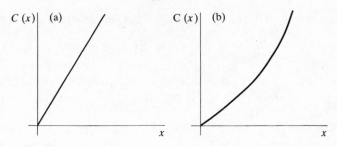

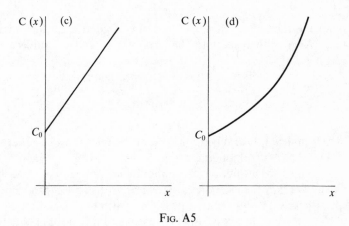

Fig. A5

which means that increasing the production from x to $x + dx$ increases the cost $C(x)$ by $q^*(1/f')\,dx$. Condition (A11) can thus be rewritten under the form

$$p^* = c(x), \qquad \text{(A11')}$$

the interpretation of which is: the profit-maximizing firm chooses a level of production where its marginal cost is equal to the price at which it sells its output.

These notions of costs are rather trivial, because there is only one input in the simple economy that we are considering. Instead, suppose for a moment that the technique for producing good X makes use of two inputs: the quantity x of X is produced from the quantitites y_x of Y and z_x of Z, a good not yet considered, according to

$$x = h(y_x, z_x). \tag{A14}$$

We assume that the production function h is increasing and differentiable in y_x and z_x. Let us then consider the following problem: one wants to produce some predetermined quantity $\tilde{x}$ of X; what mix of inputs should be used to do so?

The firm producing good X seeks to maximize its profit; hence, whatever the quantity of X produced, it seeks to minimize the cost of producing that quantity. Denote by q^* and r^* the prices at which it buys goods Y and Z; if it uses y_x units of good Y and z_x units of good Z in order to produce $\tilde{x}$ units of good X, the resulting cost is

$$q^* y_x + r^* z_x. \tag{A15}$$

Minimizing the cost of producing $\tilde{x}$ units of good X is thus minimizing (A15), with respect to the variables y_x and z_x, subject to $h(y_x, z_x) = \tilde{x}$.

A necessary condition for this constrained minimization problem is

$$\frac{\partial h / \partial y_x}{\partial h / \partial z_x} = \frac{q^*}{r^*}; \tag{A16}$$

i.e., the technical rate of substitution between inputs must be equal to the ratio of the corresponding prices.

Let $\tilde{y}_x$ and $\tilde{z}_x$ be a solution of the above constrained minimization problem. We may then say that $q^* \tilde{y}_x + r^* \tilde{z}_x$ is the cost of producing $\tilde{x}$, given prices q^* and r^*: it is possible to produce $\tilde{x}$ at that cost provided an efficient mix of inputs is used, and it is not possible to produce $\tilde{x}$ at a lower cost. In this way, we are back to the notion of cost of producing x as a well defined increasing function of x.

Let us go back to the economy with the simple production function $f(y_x)$. When the firm's maximization problem has a unique solution (as is the case in Figure A1(b), with f concave), whatever the prices p and q it faces,[16] i.e. when the production plan realized to maximize profit is uniquely determined by these prices, then it is possible to speak of an output supply function $x(p, q)$ and an input (or factor) demand function $y_x(p, q)$. For example, if (x', y'_x) is the solution at prices p^* and q^*, x' is the output supply at these prices:

$$x' = x(p^*, q^*);$$

[16] It is also possible to define the supply and demand functions on a subset of all possible prices.

and y'_x is the factor demand:

$$y'_x = y_x(p^*, q^*).$$

The firm's supply and demand functions are homogeneous of degree zero in prices: multiplying both p^* and q^* by the same positive number merely multiplies the profit by that number without changing the solutions to the constrained maximization problem (A10).

In the case depicted in Figure A1(a), one cannot speak of functions, but merely of correspondences. Indeed, for p and q such that

$\dfrac{p}{q} = \dfrac{1}{a}$, any point on the production function is a solution;

$\dfrac{p}{q} < \dfrac{1}{a}$, the origin is the only solution;

$\dfrac{p}{q} > \dfrac{1}{a}$, there is no solution.

When condition (A11) is not only a necessary condition for the constrained maximization problem (A10), but also a sufficient condition,[17] then (x^*, y^*_x) maximizes the firm's profit at prices p^* and q^*. Indeed, (x^*, y^*_x) is a solution of problem (A3); hence it satisfies condition (A8) with $p = p^*$ and $q = q^*$; i.e., it satisfies condition (A11). Thus a Pareto-efficient allocation can be implemented, as far as production is concerned, as a profit-maximizing production plan for the firm faced with suitable prices, namely p^* and q^*. It is even the only such plan if the firm's profit-maximizing problem has a unique solution; then $x' = x^* = x(p^*, q^*)$ and $y'_x = y^*_x = y_x(p^*, q^*)$.

Consumers: maximizing utility subject to a budget constraint. We now consider the consumption side. More specifically, we consider what happens if each consumer is faced with the prices p^* and q^* and is given an income equal to the value, at these prices, of the consumption bundle (x^*_A, y^*_A) or (x^*_B, y^*_B), that he gets in the Pareto-efficient allocation $(x^*_A, y^*_A, x^*_B, y^*_B)$. Take for example consumer A: he is given the income

$$R^*_A = p^* x^*_A + q^* y^*_A,$$

and, provided he does not spend more than R^*_A, he is welcome to buy at prices p^* and q^* any bundle (x_A, y_A); in other words, he is

---

[17] This is the case when f is linear or concave, as in Figure A1(a) and (b).

welcome to buy any bundle (x_A, y_A) that satisfies the budget constraint

$$p^* x_A + q^* y_A \leqslant R_A^*. \tag{A17}$$

It is clear that A can afford to buy (x_A^*, y_A^*). But is (x_A^*, y_A^*) a preferred bundle for him, among all those that satisfy the budget constraint (A17)? In other words, is (x_A^*, y_A^*) a solution to A's utility maximizing problem,[18]

$$\max U_A(x_A, y_A) \tag{A18}$$
$$\text{s.t. } R_A^* - p^* x_A - q^* y_A = 0?$$

A geometric approach immediately suggests (see Figure A6) that,

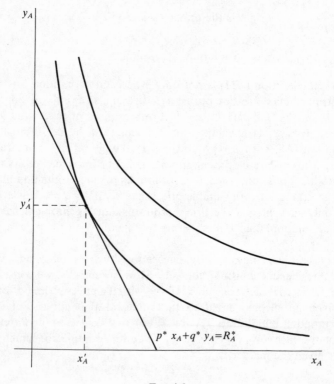

FIG. A6

---

[18] At any solution, the budget constraint must be satisfied as an equality, since U_A is increasing in x_A and y_A.

at a solution (x'_A, y'_A) of (A18), the indifference curve

$$U_A(x_A, y_A) = U_A(x'_A, y'_A)$$

is tangent to the budget constraint

$$p^* x_A + q^* y_A = R^*_A.$$

In other words, at (x'_A, y'_A) one has

$$\frac{\partial U_A/\partial x_A}{p^*} = \frac{\partial U_A/\partial y_A}{q^*}, \qquad (A19)$$

provided U_A is differentiable and x'_A and y'_A are both positive. This necessary condition is obtained in a rigorous way by deriving the Lagrangean

$$\mathscr{L}(x_A, y_A; \lambda) = U_A(x_A, y_A) + \lambda(R^*_A - p^* x_A - q^* y_A)$$

with respect to x_A and y_A.

When condition (A19) is not only a necessary condition for problem (A18), but also a sufficient condition,[19] then (x^*_A, y^*_A) is a solution of that problem. Indeed, (x^*_A, y^*_A) is a solution of problem (A3); hence it satisfies conditions (A4) and (A5) with $p = p^*$ and $q = q^*$; i.e., it satisfies (A19). Thus, (x^*_A, y^*_A) is a utility-maximizing bundle for consumer A subject to the budget constraint $p^* x_A + q^* y_A = R^*_A$. It is even the only such bundle if the utility-maximizing problem has a unique solution.

When the utility-maximizing problem has a unique solution (as is the case in Figure A6, with U_A quasi-concave), whatever the prices p and q that consumer A faces, it is possible to speak of his demand functions $x_A(p, q; R_A)$ and $y_A(p, q; R_A)$. For example, at prices p^* and q^*, A's demand functions take the values

$$x_A(p^*, q^*; R^*_A) = x^*_A \quad \text{and} \quad y_A(p^*, q^*; R^*_A) = y^*_A$$

provided (x^*_A, y^*_A) is the unique solution of problem (A18). The consumer's demand functions are homogeneous of degree zero in prices and income: multiplying p^*, q^*, and R^*_A by the same positive number does not change the utility-maximizing problem.

We could deal with consumer B in the same way, endowing him with the income

$$R^*_B = p^* x^*_B + q^* y^*_B.$$

We have

$$R^*_A + R^*_B = p^*(x^*_A + x^*_B) + q^*(y^*_A + y^*_B)$$
$$= p^* f(y^*_x) - q^* y^*_x + q^* y_0,$$

---

[19] This is the case when U_A is quasi-concave, as in Figure A6.

which means that the sum of R_A^* and R_B^* is equal to the total income available in the economy, i.e. to the sum of the firm's profit and of the value of the initial resources, both evaluated with the prices p^* and q^*. In other words, R_A^* and R_B^* represent a distribution of the total income available in the economy at the Pareto-efficient allocation $(x_A^*, y_A^*, x_B^*, y_B^*)$, with prices p^* and q^*. Summing up, with the prices p^* and q^* and the incomes R_A^* and R_B^*, it is possible to implement— as far as consumption is concerned—a Pareto-efficient allocation as a set of utility-maximizing bundles for the consumers subject to budget constraints determined by those prices and incomes.

Fundamental theorems of welfare economics. Having successively considered the production side and the consumption side of the economy, we have associated prices, namely p^* and q^*, to a Pareto-efficient allocation, namely $(x_A^*, y_A^*, x_B^*, y_B^*)$, and we have seen how these prices allow us to implement the allocation as a competitive equilibrium. Indeed, we have seen, under certain conditions, that:

1. provided each consumer, A or B, aims at maximizing his utility subject to his budget constraint, he actually maximizes his utility by choosing the consumption bundle (x_y^*, y_A^*), or (x_B^*, y_B^*), when he is faced with prices p* and q^* and is given income R_A^*, or R_B^*;
2. provided the firm that is in charge of producing good X from good Y aims at maximizing its profit subject to the prevailing technical constraint, it actually maximizes its profit by choosing the production plan (x^*, y_x^*), when it is faced with prices p^* and q^*;
3. the scarcity constraints are satisfied by consumption bundles (x_A^*, y_A^*) and (x_B^*, y_B^*); in other words, the market for each good clears, i.e. for each good total supply equals total demand.

Loosely speaking, a competitive equilibrium is defined as a set of prices[20] (one for each good in the economy), a set of consumption bundles (one for each consumer), and a set of production plans (one for each firm) such that each consumer's utility and each firm's profit is maximized subject to the relevant constraint, and such that the market for each good clears. More concisely, a competitive equilibrium is a set of prices and a set of quantities demanded or supplied

---

[20] Because the supply and demand functions are homogeneous of degree zero, multiplying all prices and incomes by the same positive number is immaterial; what matters here is relative prices, not absolute prices.

at these prices such that the market for each good clears. From this definition, and from what we have shown above, it results that, if the consumers are given incomes R_A^* and R_B^*, then p^*, q^*, (x_A^*, y_A^*), (x_B^*, y_B^*), and (x^*, y_x^*) constitute a competitive equilibrium.

Extended to an economy with any number of goods, consumers and firms, this result is called the 'second fundamental theorem of welfare economics'. It can be stated under the following form,[21] and proved without any reference to differentiability by using a separating hyperplane theorem:

Consider a Pareto-efficient allocation, the components of which are all positive; if all consumers have increasing, continuous, and quasi-concave utility functions, and if all production functions are concave,[22] then there exist a set of prices (for all goods) and a distribution among the consumers of the total income available, such that the allocation considered is a competitive equilibrium.

The prices involved are called 'competitive prices'.

The converse—that any competitive equilibrium brings about a Pareto-efficient allocation—is true under far less demanding assumptions;[23] it is called the 'first fundamental theorem of welfare economics'.

A2. Expenditure Function and Compensated Demands: Main Properties[24]

We consider a consumer who decides how much of M different private goods he will buy. These goods are offered for sale at prices p_j $(j = 1, \ldots, M)$. We will use the notations $\mathbf{p}$ for the M-vector of prices p_j and $\mathbf{x}$ for the M-vector of quantities x_j that the consumer contemplates buying. His decision results from maximizing a utility function $U(\mathbf{x})$ subject to a budget constraint $\mathbf{px} = R$, where R is his

---

[21] There are more general forms; see Varian (1984, ch. 5).

[22] Here the word 'concave' is used in a broader sense than has been the case up to now in this section: the condition for f being concave in this broader sense is $f\{\delta y' + (1 - \delta)y''\} \geqslant \delta f(y') + (1 - \delta)f(y'')$. A linear function is concave in this broader sense, while it is not in the former one.

[23] See Varian (1984, ch. 5).

[24] Here we give only a sketchy presentation of concepts and results that are needed in sec. 3 of ch. 4. For more detailed presentations, see Deaton and Muellbauer (1980), or Varian (1984).

initial income:[25]

$$\max_{\mathbf{x}} U(\mathbf{x}) \tag{A20}$$

$$\text{s.t. } \mathbf{px} = R.$$

We will always assume that U is quasi-concave, differentiable, and increasing in each x_j. Solving (A20) gives the vector of demand functions $\mathbf{x}(\mathbf{p}, R)$, which expresses the consumer's decision as a function of prices and initial income. Consider then the function $V(\mathbf{p}, R)$ of prices and income, which is derived from the direct utility function $U(\mathbf{x})$ by substituting for $\mathbf{x}$ the optimal decision, given prices $\mathbf{p}$ and income R:

$$V(\mathbf{p}, R) = U\{\mathbf{x}(\mathbf{p}, R)\}. \tag{A21}$$

$V(\mathbf{p}, R)$ is an indirect utility function which indicates how the consumer ranks the various pairs $(\mathbf{p}, R)$.

In (A20), the consumer is faced with prices $\mathbf{p}$, he has a fixed income R to spend, and he maximizes utility. Let us now consider a dual approach: a level u of utility is set and the consumer, who is still faced with prices $\mathbf{p}$, minimizes expenditure:

$$\min_{\mathbf{x}} \mathbf{px} \tag{A22}$$

$$\text{s.t. } U(\mathbf{x}) = u.$$

Solving (A22) gives the vector of compensated demand functions $\mathbf{x}^c(\mathbf{p}, u)$; they are compensated in the sense that, in order to remain at the level u of utility, the consumer must be compensated in terms of initial income for changes in $\mathbf{p}$. The consumer's expenditure function is then the minimum income that he must have available to reach the utility level u when buying at prices $\mathbf{p}$:

$$e(\mathbf{p}, u) = \mathbf{px}^c(\mathbf{p}, u). \tag{A23}$$

Both approaches are connected in the following way: consider a fixed value R of the initial income, and the corresponding level $V(\mathbf{p}, R)$ of utility. Then, if u is chosen as $u = V(\mathbf{p}, R)$, the compensated demands $\mathbf{x}^c(\mathbf{p}, u)$ are equal to the ordinary demands $\mathbf{x}(\mathbf{p}, R)$ and the expenditure function $e(\mathbf{p}, u)$ takes the value R:

$$u = V(\mathbf{p}, R) \quad \text{or} \quad R = e(\mathbf{p}, u) \tag{A24}$$

---

[25] If one among the M goods is used as numeraire, i.e. if its price is always kept equal to 1, then R is measured in that good.

and
$$\mathbf{x}^c\{\mathbf{p}, V(\mathbf{p}, R)\} = \mathbf{x}(\mathbf{p}, R) \quad \text{or} \quad \mathbf{x}\{\mathbf{p}, e(\mathbf{p}, u)\} = \mathbf{x}^c(\mathbf{p}, u). \quad \text{(A25)}$$

It is worth stressing that, even when R and u are connected by (A24), $\mathbf{x}(\mathbf{p}, R)$ and $\mathbf{x}^c(\mathbf{p}, u)$ have derivatives with respect to the prices that in general are different:

$$\frac{\partial \mathbf{x}(\mathbf{p}, R)}{\partial p_j} \neq \frac{\partial \mathbf{x}^c(\mathbf{p}, u)}{\partial p_j}.$$

We will see later how these derivatives are related (Slutsky conditions). However, when U takes the particular form

$$U(\mathbf{x}) = u(x_1, \ldots, x_{m-1}) + x_m$$

and good m is used as numeraire, the ordinary and compensated demand functions for goods 1 to $m - 1$ are identical; they depend neither on R nor on u.

The expenditure function has the following properties:

— it is increasing in prices and in utility level;
— it is homogeneous of degree one in prices;
— it is concave in prices;
— it has first and second partial derivatives with respect to prices.[26]

These derivatives themselves have useful properties, which are gathered in the three following propositions.

PROPOSITION 1. The first derivatives of the expenditure function with respect to prices are the compensated demands:

$$\frac{\partial e(\mathbf{p}, u)}{\partial p_j} = x_j^c(\mathbf{p}, u), \quad j = 1, \ldots, M. \quad \text{(A26)}$$

This results almost immediately from the definitions. Let indeed $\mathbf{q}$ be any price vector (hence, in general different from $\mathbf{p}$). Let $\mathbf{x}$ be any consumption vector such that $U(\mathbf{x}) = u$. From the definition of the expenditure function, we have

$$\mathbf{q}\mathbf{x} - e(\mathbf{q}, u) \geq 0.$$

This is true in particular for $\mathbf{x} = \mathbf{x}^c(\mathbf{p}, u)$:

$$\mathbf{q}\mathbf{x}^c(\mathbf{p}, u) - e(\mathbf{q}, u) \geq 0.$$

[26] When the direct utility function U is continuous but not differentiable, this property is somewhat weaker: the expenditure function has first and second partial derivatives for almost all price vectors.

The left-hand side of this last inequality is a differentiable function of $\mathbf{q}$ that reaches a minimum at $\mathbf{q} = \mathbf{p}$; the derivatives of this function with respect to q_j $(j = 1, \ldots, M)$ are thus zero at $\mathbf{q} = \mathbf{p}$:

$$x_j^c(\mathbf{p}, u) - \left\{ \frac{\partial e(\mathbf{q}, u)}{\partial q_j} \right\}_{\mathbf{q} = \mathbf{p}} = 0$$

or

$$\frac{\partial e(\mathbf{p}, u)}{\partial p_j} = x_j^c(\mathbf{p}, u).$$

PROPOSITION 2. The Slutsky matrix of the first derivatives of the compensated demands with respect to prices, is symmetric and semi-definite negative.

The Slutsky matrix is indeed the matrix of the second derivatives of the expenditure function, which is concave in prices.

PROPOSITION 3. For $u = V(\mathbf{p}, R)$, the first derivatives of the ordinary and compensated demands with respect to prices are related by the Slutsky conditions; i.e., they satisfy

$$\frac{\partial x_i^c}{\partial p_j} = \frac{\partial x_i}{\partial p_j} + x_j \frac{\partial x_i}{\partial R}, \quad i \text{ and } j = 1, \ldots, M. \tag{A27}$$

Indeed, as $u = V(\mathbf{p}, R)$, we have, from (A25),

$$x_i^c(\mathbf{p}, u) = x_i\{\mathbf{p}, e(\mathbf{p}, u)\}.$$

Hence

$$\frac{\partial x_i^c}{\partial p_j} = \frac{\partial x_i}{\partial p_j} + \frac{\partial x_i}{\partial R} \frac{\partial e}{\partial p_j} = \frac{\partial x_i}{\partial p_j} + \frac{\partial x_i}{\partial R} x_j^c$$

$$= \frac{\partial x_i}{\partial p_j} + \frac{\partial x_i}{\partial R} x_j.$$

A fourth proposition proves useful. It is about the derivatives of the indirect utility function, and it is known as Roy's Identity. It is a kind of counterpart for the indirect utility function of proposition 1 for the expenditure function.

PROPOSITION 4. The first derivatives of the indirect utility function with respect to prices are the ordinary demands multiplied by the opposite of the marginal utility of income:

$$\frac{\partial V}{\partial p_j} = -x_j \frac{\partial V}{\partial R}, \quad j = 1, \ldots, M. \tag{A28}$$

Choosing $u = V(\mathbf{p}, R)$, we can indeed write

$$u = V\{\mathbf{p}, e(\mathbf{p}, u)\}.$$

Deriving this identity with respect to p_j gives

$$0 = \frac{\partial V}{\partial p_j} + \frac{\partial V}{\partial R} \frac{\partial e}{\partial p_j}$$

$$= \frac{\partial V}{\partial p_j} + \frac{\partial V}{\partial R} x_j.$$

We will complete this section by considering an indirect utility function that is sometimes called 'money metric utility', or 'equivalent income', because it is measured in the same unit as income. Let U be a direct utility function for the consumer and V the corresponding indirect utility function. Let also $\mathbf{p}$ and $\mathbf{q}$ be two price vectors. Then, as the expenditure function is increasing in the utility level, the function

$$\Psi(\mathbf{q}; \mathbf{p}, R) = e\{\mathbf{q}, V(\mathbf{p}, R)\}, \tag{A29}$$

when considered as a function of $\mathbf{p}$ and $R(\mathbf{q})$ is then considered as a reference price, i.e. a parameter), is another indirect utility function, equivalent to V. Definition (A29) can also be given under the form

$$V(\mathbf{q}, \Psi) = V(\mathbf{p}, R), \tag{A30}$$

which says that Ψ is the minimum initial income necessary to reach the utility level $V(\mathbf{p}, R)$ when prices are $\mathbf{q}$.

The last concept we consider is the equivalent lump-sum contribution:

$$\phi(\mathbf{q}; \mathbf{p}, R) = R - \Psi(\mathbf{q}; \mathbf{p}, R). \tag{A31}$$

In order to bring out its meaning, let us consider three hypothetic situations. In situation A, the consumer has the initial income R and is faced with prices $\mathbf{q}$. Situation B' is derived from A by changing $\mathbf{q}$ into $\mathbf{p}$, R being invariant. Situation B'' is derived from A by changing R into $R - \phi$, $\mathbf{q}$ being invariant. From (A30) and (A31), it is immediately seen that the consumer is indifferent between B' and B'', hence is indifferent between moving from A to B' or from A to B''. It thus appears that deducting ϕ from the initial income R as a lump-sum contribution (keeping $\mathbf{q}$ as price vector) has the same effect on the consumer's utility as changing the price vector from $\mathbf{q}$ to $\mathbf{p}$ (keeping R as initial income).

When U takes the particular form $U(\mathbf{x}) = u(x_1, \ldots, x_{m-1}) + x_m$ and good m is used as numeraire, the equivalent lump-sum contribution is equal to the difference between the surplus at prices $\mathbf{q}$ and the surplus at prices $\mathbf{p}$.

A3. Choices in the Presence of Risk[27]

We consider an agent A who faces a risk stemming from a random variable x, taking—as in Section 3 of Chapter 6—the value x_1 $(0 < x_1)$ with probability $1 - \pi$, and the value x_2 $(0 < x_2 < x_1)$ with probability π, where $\pi < (1 - \pi)$. In this section, we take π as a fixed parameter, whereas we allow x_1 and x_2 to vary. In the plane represented in Figure A7, let X designate the point with coordinates x_1 and x_2; X^0 for example is the point with coordinates x_1^0 and x_2^0, $\hat{X}$ the point with coordinates $\hat{x}_1$ and $\hat{x}_2$. We assume that agent A is able to compare different points, X^0 and $\hat{X}$ for example; that is to say, he is able to decide whether he prefers the prospect of having x_1^0 with probability $1 - \pi$, and x_2^0 with probability π, to the prospect of having $\hat{x}_1$ with probability $1 - \pi$ and $\hat{x}_2$ with probability π. We assume that A's preferences can be represented by some utility function $U(X) = U(x_1, x_2)$.

We say that A is risk-neutral—a possible attitude with respect to risk—if he appraises the random variable x solely on the basis of its expected value, $E[x] = (1 - \pi)x_1 + \pi x_2$. In other words, A is risk-neutral if his utility function $U(X)$ is of the form

$$U(X) = E[x]. \tag{A32}$$

An indifference curve of A is then a straight line of equation $E[x] = k$, with k a constant; examples of such indifference curves are the lines $B_1 B_2$ and $C_1 C_2$ (with slope $-(1 - \pi)/\pi$) in Figure A7.

On the other hand, an indifference curve like $\Gamma_1 \Gamma_2$ depicts risk aversion. Even though $E[x^0]$ is strictly greater than d, point D is indifferent to point X^0. D does not involve any risk since its two coordinates are equal to d, while $x_2^0 < x_1^0$. That A is risk-averse means that his utility function is no longer linear in X, but is quasi-

[27] Only a few points from this vast subject are introduced; they have been selected in order to facilitate the reading of sec. 3 in ch. 6. For a systematic presentation, see Hirschleifer and Riley (1979).

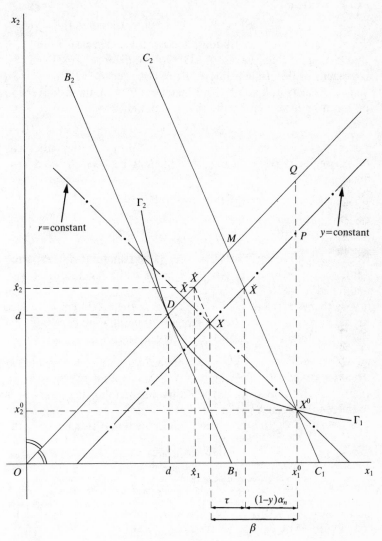

F$_{\text{IG}}$. A7

concave. It has been shown[28] that, under reasonable assumptions, there exists a numerical function v such that the utility function U can be written

$$U(X) = E[v(x)] = (1 - \pi)v(x_1) + \pi v(x_2) \qquad (A33)$$

where v is bounded, continuous, and concave. It is clear from (A33) that, at a point D on the bisector OQ, an indifference curve like $\Gamma_1 \Gamma_2$ is tangent to the straight line $B_1 B_2$ of equation $E[x] = d$.

The intensity at a point X, for instance at X^0, of the risk aversion of A can be measured by the risk premium[29]

$$\varrho = E[x^0] - d. \qquad (A34)$$

From (A34), ϱ appears as the length of the projection on either axis of the segment DM. That A is indifferent between X^0 and D is written

$$U(X^0) = U(D),$$

or

$$E[v(x^0)] = v(E[x^0] - \varrho), \qquad (A35)$$

from which it is clearly seen that ϱ is the maximum loss in expected value that A is ready to accept in order to be relieved of all risk embodied in x^0.

Whether A is risk-neutral or risk-averse, the maximum insurance premium α that he is ready to pay, for obtaining full coverage[30] of the risk embodied in x^0, is defined by the equation

$$E[v(x^0)] = v(x_1^0 - \alpha). \qquad (A36)$$

This is another way of saying that A is indifferent between X^0 (with risk) or D (without risk), but this time in the following terms: A is indifferent between $X^0 = (x_1^0, x_2^0)$ or $D = (x_1^0 - \alpha, x_2^0 - \alpha + \gamma)$, with $\gamma = L = x_1^0 - x_2^0$. In other words, A is indifferent between risking the

---

[28] By J. von Neumann and O. Morgenstern, in *Theory of Games and Economic Behavior*, 1944; v is thus called a von Neumann–Morgenstern function. It is a random function, since the value it takes is determined by the value that the random variable x takes. For more details, and especially the proof of the theorem, see Malinvaud (1985). If not only x but also the structure of the preferences of A are contingent on the same random event, then (A33) is no longer true. However, it has been shown by Hirschleifer (1965) that, under relatively mild assumptions, the utility function U can be written

$$U(X) = (1 - \pi)v_1(x_1) + \pi v_2(x_2),$$

where a different numerical function v_i is associated with each possible outcome.

[29] Which should not be confused with an insurance premium.

[30] To obtain full coverage means that a point on the bisector OQ is substituted for X^0.

loss $L = x_1^0 - x_2^0$ or subscribing an insurance contract providing for the payment of α to the insurer, whatever the outcome of the random event, and the payment of γ by the insurer, upon occurrence of the loss.[31] We call γ the 'indemnity'; that it is equal to the loss L means that the contract offers full coverage. From (A35) and (A36), we immediately derive

$$\alpha = \alpha_n + \varrho$$

where

$$\alpha_n = \pi L$$

is the particular value that α takes for a risk-neutral agent. From the previous definitions, α_n appears as the length of the projection on either axis of the segment MQ, and α as the length of the projection on either axis of the segment DQ.

All the points of the bisector OQ in Figure A7, like $\tilde{X}$ for example, correspond to insurance contracts with full coverage: for point X^0, such that $x_2^0 < x_1^0$, point $\tilde{X}$ is substituted, such that $\tilde{x}_1 = \tilde{x}_2$. Points like X or $\check{X}$, on the other hand, correspond to contracts with partial coverage, or in other words contracts involving a deductible: for point X^0, for example, point X is substituted such that $0 < x_1 - x_2 < x_1^0 - x_2^0$. The insurance premium β, the indemnity γ, the deductible yL, and the insurer's profit τ,[32] which are attached to X, are defined by the equations

$$x_1 = x_1^0 - \beta \tag{A37}$$

$$x_2 = x_2^0 - \beta + \gamma \tag{A38}$$

$$x_1 - x_2 = yL \tag{A39}$$

$$\tau = \beta - \pi\gamma. \tag{A40}$$

We will call y the 'rate of self-insurance'. Also, we will call $1 - y$ the 'rate of coverage', because

$$\gamma = (1 - y)L. \tag{A41}$$

---

[31] The payment of α is sure, whereas the payment of γ is contingent upon an outcome of the random event.

[32] The profit τ is the average profit over a sufficiently large set of contracts which are all identical to X but are subscribed by agents exposed to stochastically well adapted random events. The best known variety of stochastically well adapted random events is that of stochastically independent random events; but the former is considerably broader, as shown in Revesz (1968).

In Section 3 of Chapter 6, we make use of the following simple results:

— the insurance premium is the same at all the points of *a* parallel to the axis Ox_2;
— the indemnity is the same at all the points of *a* parallel to the bisector *OQ*;
— the deductible is the same at all the points of *a* parallel to the bisector *OQ*;
— the ratio *r* of the indemnity to the premium is the same at all the points of *a* straight line passing through X^0, and the slope of this line is equal to $1 - r$;

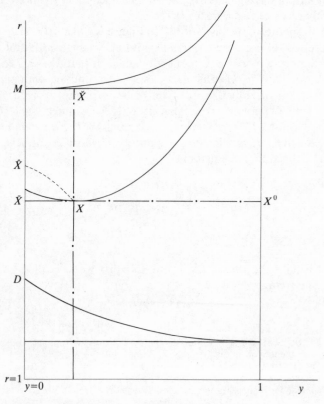

FIG. A8

— the profit τ is the same at all the points of a parallel to the straight line $X^0 M$, and agent A's utility is strictly increasing in the direction from X^0 up to M.

The third and fourth of these results make it useful to work in the plane (y, r) instead of the plane (x_1, x_2). For this reason, we have transformed Figure A7, which is drawn in the plane (x_1, x_2), into Figure A8, which is its image in the plane (y, r).

References

Atkinson, A., and Stiglitz, J. (1980), *Lectures on Public Economics*, McGraw Hill, New York.

Baumol, W. J. (1982), 'Contestable Markets: An Uprising in the Theory of Industry Structure', *American Economic Review*, 72: 1–15.

—— and Willig, R. D. (1986), 'Contestability: Developments since the Book', *Oxford Economic Papers*, 38 (Supplementary Issue): 9–36.

Bohm, P. (1972), 'Estimating Demand for Public Goods: An Experiment', *European Economic Review*, 3: 111–30.

—— (1984), 'Revealing Demand for an Actual Public Good', *Journal of Public Economics*, 24: 135–52.

Boiteux, M. (1956), 'Sur la question des monopoles publics astreints à l'équilibre budgétaire', *Econometrica*, 24: 22–40; English translation (1971) in *Journal of Economic Theory*, 3: 219–40.

Bös, D. (1985), 'Public sector pricing', in A. J. Auerbach and M. Feldstein (eds.), *Handbook of Public Economics*, Vol. 1, North-Holland, Amsterdam.

Bosselman, F., Callies, D., and Bania, J. (1973), *The Taking Issue*, US Government Printing Office, Washington, DC.

Champsaur, P., Drèze, J. H., and Henry, C. (1977), 'Stability Theorems with Economic Applications', *Econometrica*, 45: 273–94.

Cornes, R., and Sandler, T. (1986), *The Theory of Externalities, Public Goods, and Club Goods*, Cambridge University Press.

Deaton, A., and Muellbauer, J. (1980), *Economics and Consumer Behavior*, Cambridge University Press.

Debreu, G. (1954), 'Representation of a Preference Ordering by a Numerical Function', in R. M. Thrall, C. H. Coombs, and R. C. Davis (eds.), *Decision Processes*, John Wiley, New York.

GAO (1982), *A Market Approach to Air Pollution Control Could Reduce Compliance Costs without Jeopardizing Clean Air Goals*, GAO, Washington, DC.

Glaister, S. (1976), 'Peak Load Pricing and the Channel Tunnel', *Journal of Transport Economics and Policy*, 10: 99–112.

—— (1981), *Fundamentals of Transport Economics*, Basil Blackwell, Oxford.

Green, J., and Laffont, J. J. (1979), *Individual Incentives in Public Decision-making*, North-Holland, Amsterdam.

Guesnerie, R. (1980), 'Second-best Pricing Rules in the Boiteux Tradition: Derivation, Review and Discussion', *Journal of Public Economics*, 13: 51–80.

Hagen, K. P. (1979), 'Optimal Pricing in Public Firms in an Imperfect Market Economy', *Scandinavian Journal of Economics*, 81: 475–93.

Henriet, D., Henry, C., Rey, P., and Rochet, J. C. (1988), 'Intérêt public, intérêt privé et discrimination', *L'Actualité économique*, 63: 98–117.

Henry, C., and Zylberberg, A. (1978), 'Planning Algorithms to Deal with Increasing Returns', *Review of Economic Studies*, 45: 67–75.

Hirschleifer, J. (1965), 'The Investment Decision under Uncertainty: Choice-theoretic Approaches', *Quarterly Journal of Economics*, 79: 509–36.

—— and Riley, J. G. (1979), 'The Analytics of Uncertainty and Information: An Expository Survey', *Journal of Economic Literature*, 17: 1375–1421.

Holmes, P., (1980), '*The State and the Railways*, translation of L. Walras's *L'Etat et les chemins de fer*', *Journal of Public Economics*, 13: 81–100.

Kahn, A. A. (1966), 'The Tyranny of Small Decisions: Market Failures, Imperfections, and the Limits of Economics', *Kyklos*, 19: 23–47.

Laffont, J. J. and Maskin, E. (1982), 'The Theory of Incentives: An Overview', in W. Hildenbrand (ed.), *Advances in Economic Theory*, Cambridge University Press.

Malinvaud, E. (1985), *Lectures on Microeconomic Theory*, North-Holland, Amsterdam.

Milleron, J. C. (1972), 'Theory of Value with Public Goods: A Survey Article', *Journal of Economic Theory*, 5: 419–77.

Moulin, H. (1982), *Game Theory for the Social Sciences*, New York University Press.

Musgrave, R. A., and Peacock, A. T. (eds.) (1958), *Classics in the Theory of Public Finance*, Macmillan, London.

OECD (1975), *The Polluter-Pays Principle: Definition, Analysis, Implementation*, Paris, OECD.

Phlips, L. (1983), *The Economics of Price Discrimination*, Cambridge University Press.

Ramsey, F. (1927), 'A Contribution to the Theory of Taxation', *Economic Journal*, 37: 47–61.

Revesz, P. (1968), *The Laws of Large Numbers*, Academic Press, New York.

Salop, S. (1977), 'The Noisy Monopolist: Imperfect Information, Price Dispersion, and Price Discrimination', *Review of Economic Studies*, 44: 393–406.

Samuelson, P. A. (1954), 'The Pure Theory of Public Expenditure', *Review of Economics and Statistics*, 36: 387–9.

Spence, A. M. (1974), *Market Signaling: Informational Transfer in Hiring and Related Screening Processes*, Harvard University Press, Cambridge, Mass.

Varian, H. R. (1984), *Microeconomic Analysis*, W. W. Norton, New York.

—— (1987). *Intermediate Microeconomics: A Modern Approach*, W. W. Norton, New York.

Waterson, M. (1987), 'Recent Developments in the Theory of Natural Monopoly', *Journal of Economic Surveys*, 1: 59–80.

Index